Seventy Years of Blackness

the Autobiography of Verda Byrd
As told to Joyce Garlick-Peavy

Seventy Years of Blackness

the Autobiography of Verda Byrd
As told to Joyce Garlick-Peavy

Harrison House Publishing

Cover photo by R40 Photo & Media Group
Converse, TX 78109
210-833-1975

Cover Design by GenesisProDesigns.com

Harrison House Publishing
www.theharrisonhousepublishing.com
info@theharrisonhousepublising.com
ISBN: 978-0-9974935-8-0
Library of Congress Control Number: 2017950975
Harrison House Publishing and the "HH" logo are trademarks belonging to Harrison House Publishing.

PRINTED IN THE UNITED STATES OF AMERICA

DEDICATION

Verda Byrd dedicates her autobiography, *Seventy Years of Blackness*, to the following:

➢ **First**, her loving mother, Daisy Beagle who made the decision to make sure her daughter would have the amenities in life to support her growth

➢ **Second**, her loving parents, Edwinna and Ray Wagner

➢ **Third**, all new and accepted family members; and

➢ **Fourth**, my loving husband and daughter who have been with me "every step of the way."

Verda closes her dedication with, "I would like to thank my husband Trancle Byrd for his loving support in my personal journey. Thank you all with forever love; Jeanette Beagle aka Verda Ann Wagner Byrd."

PREFACE

This is the true story of an adoptee that spent her first few years not knowing she was adopted. Today, that individual, Verda Byrd lives in San Antonio, Texas. Verda was legally adopted at the age of five by a Negro family. She was born in 1942; in 1943 she was placed in the foster care system in Kansas City, Missouri; her place of birth.

In 1947, Verda was adopted by Ray and Edwinna Wagner (see copy of attached adoption document). The Wagner's were an affluent Negro family, able to provide all the amenities that their only child needed. At age 10 her parents, the Wagners, told Verda she was adopted. The significance of being adopted had no meaning to her and she did not realize what this implied.

Verda's family was very religious always attending church—traditionally Black church. Today Verda continues to attend a Black church.

Now we move forward in Verda's life a time after her adoptive parents were deceased. It was while going through the family's paperwork Verda was in for the surprise of her life. As you read through this heart-warming story you will get an understanding of the feeling—being born White, adopted and raised by a "Negro" (the term used on the birth record) couple and at age 70 finding out that you are really "White!"

Having spent seventy years as a Negro, Verda thought I have been in "Seventy Years of Blackness." Blackness as defined by *The Free* Dictionary is "1) the quality or state of being black; and 2) the quality or state of being a black person." Go with Verda on this amazing journey as she discovers her roots.

**Many of the documents you will view in this book are from the originals which are more than 70 years old.

CONTENTS

THE EARLY YEARS

Verda Byrd was born on September 27, 1942, the fifth child of Daisy and Earl Beagle, in Kansas City, Missouri. She does not know the place of birth e.g., hospital. Verda's birth name was Jeanette Beagle. Her name was changed to Verda Ann Wagner when she was adopted. The first five years of Verda's life are very vague. Based on research it was found that Verda was placed in the welfare system in Kansas City, Missouri in February 1943. On January 14, 1944 consent to adopt a minor was signed by Verda's birth mother, Daisy Beagle. Prior to adoption, Verda was in the welfare system for approximately one year before she was eligible for foster care and adoption.

The Biological Parents—the Beagles

Jeanette Beagle was the fifth living child of Daisy and Earl Beagle. Daisy and Earl Beagle were White Americans. A copy of their photograph is attached. Also, census information confirming their birth, race, and death are attached.

Daisy and Earl Beagle (Biological Parents)

Note: *The Ancestry.com website will undergo scheduled maintenance on Monday, 24 February, from approximately 1 a.m. to 8 a.m. (EST). During that time, some portions of the site may be unavailable. Thank you for your patience.*

Note: *This site uses cookies to help manage and personalize your visits to Ancestry. By using the site, you agree to our use of cookies. Learn More.*

ancestry.com   2   verdabyrd42 ⌄   Upgrade   Get help

| Home | Family Trees ⌄ | Search | DNA ⌄ | Collaborate ⌄ | Learning Center ⌄ | Publish | Shop | Hire An Expert |

Provided in Association with THE NATIONAL ARCHIVES

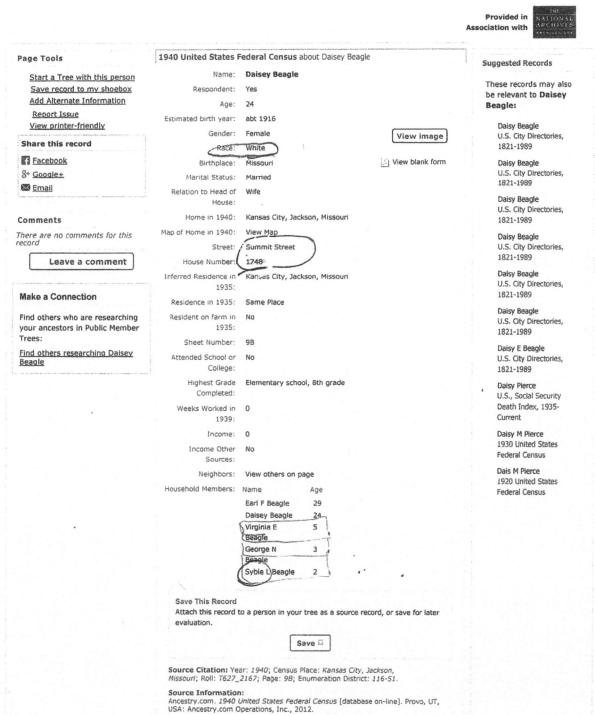

Page Tools

Start a Tree with this person
Save record to my shoebox
Add Alternate Information
Report Issue
View printer-friendly

Share this record

Facebook
Google+
Email

Comments

There are no comments for this record

Leave a comment

Make a Connection

Find others who are researching your ancestors in Public Member Trees:

Find others researching Daisey Beagle

1940 United States Federal Census about Daisey Beagle

Name:	**Daisey Beagle**
Respondent:	Yes
Age:	24
Estimated birth year:	abt 1916
Gender:	Female
Race:	White
Birthplace:	Missouri
Marital Status:	Married
Relation to Head of House:	Wife
Home in 1940:	Kansas City, Jackson, Missouri
Map of Home in 1940:	View Map
Street:	Summit Street
House Number:	1748
Inferred Residence in 1935:	Kansas City, Jackson, Missouri
Residence in 1935:	Same Place
Resident on farm in 1935:	No
Sheet Number:	9B
Attended School or College:	No
Highest Grade Completed:	Elementary school, 8th grade
Weeks Worked in 1939:	0
Income:	0
Income Other Sources:	No
Neighbors:	View others on page

View image

View blank form

Suggested Records

These records may also be relevant to **Daisey Beagle:**

Daisy Beagle
U.S. City Directories, 1821-1989

Daisy Beagle
U.S. City Directories, 1821-1989

Daisy Beagle
U.S. City Directories, 1821-1989

Daisy Beagle
U.S. City Directories, 1821-1989

Daisy Beagle
U.S. City Directories, 1821-1989

Daisy Beagle
U.S. City Directories, 1821-1989

Daisy E Beagle
U.S. City Directories, 1821-1989

Daisy Pierce
U.S., Social Security Death Index, 1935-Current

Daisy M Pierce
1930 United States Federal Census

Dais M Pierce
1920 United States Federal Census

Household Members:

Name	Age
Earl F Beagle	29
Daisey Beagle	24
Virginia E Beagle	5
George N Beagle	3
Syble L Beagle	2

Save This Record
Attach this record to a person in your tree as a source record, or save for later evaluation.

Save

Source Citation: Year: *1940*; Census Place: *Kansas City, Jackson, Missouri*; Roll: *T627_2167*; Page: *9B*; Enumeration District: *116-51*.

Source Information:
Ancestry.com. *1940 United States Federal Census* [database on-line]. Provo, UT, USA: Ancestry.com Operations, Inc., 2012.

ancestry.com

2

verdabyrd42 ▾   Upgrade   Get Help

Home | Family Trees ▾ | Search | DNA ▾ | Collaborate ▾ | Learning Center ▾ | Publish | Shop | Hire An Expert

Page Tools

Start a Tree with this person
Save record to my shoebox
Add Alternate Information
☒ Order Original Document
View printer-friendly
☒ Request copy of original application

Comments

There are no comments for this record

Leave a comment

Make a Connection

Find others who are researching your ancestors in Public Member Trees:

Find others researching Daisy Pierce

U.S., Social Security Death Index, 1935-Current about Daisy Pierce

Name:	**Daisy Pierce**
SSN:	~~██████~~
Last Residence:	75246 Dallas, Dallas, Texas, USA
BORN:	6 Aug 1915
Died:	18 Sep 2002
State (Year) SSN issued:	Missouri (Before 1951)

Save This Record
Attach this record to a person in your tree as a source record, or save for later evaluation.

Save ▾

Source Citation: Number: *500-22-9969*; Issue State: *Missouri*; Issue Date: *Before 1951*.

Source Information:
Ancestry.com. *U.S., Social Security Death Index, 1935-Current* [database on-line]. Provo, UT, USA: Ancestry.com Operations Inc, 2011.
Original data: Social Security Administration. *Social Security Death Index, Master File.* Social Security Administration.

Description:
The Social Security Administration Death Master File contains information on millions of deceased individuals with United States social security numbers whose deaths were reported to the Social Security Administration. Birth years for the individuals listed range from 1875 to last year. Information in these records includes name, birth date, death date, and last known residence. Learn more...

Suggested Records

These records may also be relevant to **Daisy Pierce:**

Daisy M Pierce
1930 United States Federal Census

Dais M Pierce
1920 United States Federal Census

Daisey Beagle
1940 United States Federal Census

CRAINEY-CEY

[EL]A Y. of Dallas, age [...] September 17, [...] Viewing Friday Sep[...] [...]er 20, 2002 11 a.m. to [...]m. @ The Major Fu[...]d Home The wake: [...]y, September 20, [...] 7-8 p.m. Abundant [...] C.O.G.I.C. 3930 N. [...]pton Rd Dallas, TX. [...]rial Service Saturday [...]ember 21, 2002 at 1 [...] @ True Vine Holy [...]ple 1611 E. Ann A[...]ve Dallas TX Ser[...] Entrusted to:

The Major Funeral Home
4228 S. Lancaster Rd.
[...], Texas 75216   214.374.5900

cNEW

[...] LESTER DOYNE, [...] of Commerce, sur[...]ed by: wife, Norma [...] New of Commerce; [...] Dr. Barry McNew [...] wife Dinah of Green[...]le; daughters, Dr. Mar[...] Fitte and husband [...] of Greenville and [...]sha Hill and husband [...] of Golden, Colorado; [...]ther, Dr. Ben McNew [...]

RICHARD FOREST

Born April 6, 1948 in Dallas, Texas. Died at his home in Hopewell, Virginia, September 11, 2002. Son of Wiley Forest (deceased) and Zelta Handsky Nanney. Graduated from Lancaster High School, joined Navy serving in Pacific. Joined Army and stationed in Hawaii, Germany and retired from Ft. Lee, Virginia in 1991. Survived by Mother, Zelta Nanney of Arlington, Texas; sister Suzan Nanney of Arlington, Texas; step-sons Steven Harmon and family of Chesterfield, Virginia; Scott Harmon of Hopewell, Virginia. Memorials to your choice or Veterans Memorial Library, 1600 Veterans Parkway, Lancaster, Texas 75134.

Pickvance Sr.

COL. WILLIAM W., USAF (Ret.) 79. who died Tuesday, September 17, 2002 at his residence in Gainesville, Texas. Funeral services will be held at 2:30 p.m. on Friday, September 20th in the Dannel Funeral Home Chapel. Chaplain Ziegler of the United States Air Force will officiate. Interment will follow at West Hill Cemetery with full military honors.

Dannel Funeral Home
382 S. Walnut
Sherman, Texas 75090
903-893-1171

[...] P.U. BOX 15095, 5600 Wichita Street, Fort Worth, Texas 76119; American Red Cross, Dallas Area Chapter, 4800 Harry Hines Blvd., Dallas, TX 75235-7717; or a charity of choice.

PIERCE

DAISY, born Aug. 5, 1915 in Joplin, MO, passed away Sept. 18, 2002 in Dallas at the age of 87. She is survived by 4 daughters:

[...] grandchildren, Carrie Molina, Terrell Pierce, Eddie Rouillard, Anthony Rouillard and Danny Caldwell; 14 great-grandchildren. Funeral services will be held at 1:30 PM Monday, Sept. 23 at the Heritage Funeral Home Chapel with Elder Leonard Willis officiating. Interment will follow at Calvary Hill Memorial Park. The family will receive friends from 6:00 PM to 9:00 PM Sunday evening at the funeral home. She is loved very much and will be missed dearly. We love you Mom and Grandma!

HERITAGE FUNERAL HOME
Dallas, TX   214-333-2323

RITGER

SHIRLEY W., born September 20, 1922 in Cleveland, Mississippi, the daughter of William Bernard and Virgie Middleton Woodyear, died on September 19, 2002 in Dallas, Texas. She moved to Dallas in 1976 after living in El Dorado, Arkansas for 28 years. In El Dorado, she was an active member of First Baptist Church, the Charity League, and various civic organizations and served as a Girl Scout leader. In Dallas, she was a member of First Baptist Church of Richardson, Town North Women's Club, and Fretz Park Senior Center. She is survived by her husband of 58 years Andrew G. Ritger, Sr., her daughters and sons-in-law Holly and David M. Sudbury, Robin and Thomas T. Milam of Grass Valley, California, her son and daughter-in-law Andrew G. Ritger, Jr. and Elizabeth Branham, five grandchildren, Erin Sudbury and Gregory Sudbury of Dallas, Lila Ritger, Andrew G. Ritger, III, and Charles Ritger of Edmond, Oklahoma. Memorial Service will be held at Cox Chapel of Highland Park United Methodist Church in Dallas on Friday, September [...]

[...] Faith, [...] Reece, Matthew, [...] Robert, Brett, Brian, Matthew, Elizabeth and Bryce, sister Eunice and husband R.B. Cooper, many other nieces, nephews and cousins. Family will receive friends on Friday, September 20, 2002 from 6-8 P.M. Funeral services will be held in the chapel of Grove Hill Funeral Home on Saturday, September 21, 2002 at 10:00 A.M.

GROVE HILL
Dignity
3920 Samuell Blvd., Dallas
(214) 388-8887

SEPULVEDA

GASPAR GUSTAVO, was born on October 9, 1927 in Nuevo Laredo, Mexico and to our sorrow he passed away September 15, 2002. He is survived by his loving and devoted wife of 41 years, Maria Guadalupe Sepulveda, 5 sons; Gaspar and wife, Rosalva, Ricardo and wife, Cheryl, Roberto, Gustavo and Jorge and 2 daughters; Genoveva Nannapaneni and husband, Muralidhar and Lupita White and husband, Michael. We will remember his keen sense of hu[...]

LAU[...]

Funeral [...] 12549 [...] Mesquit[...]

SPA[...]

NITA, [...] forme[...] reside[...] 19, 20[...] [...]derga[...] school[...] eral y[...] memb[...] tist Cl[...] Surviv[...] Gene[...] Bever[...] TX; so[...] David [...] Carro[...] Spark[...] Edith [...] son, [...] and M[...] of La[...] Lillian [...] seven[...] one gr[...] ly wil[...] 8 p.m [...] neral [...] servic[...] at t[...] Churc[...] Rev. [...] ating. [...] 11 a.m [...] Fort V[...] etery. [...]

las, Texas. Died at his home in Hopewell, Virginia, September 11, 2002. Son of Wiley Forest (deceased) and Zelta Handshy Nanney. Graduated from Lancaster High School, joined Navy serving in Pacific. Joined Army and stationed in Hawaii, Germany and retired from Ft. Lee, Virginia in 1991. Survived by Mother, Zelta Nanney of Arlington, Texas; sister Susan Nanney of Arlington, Texas; step-sons Steven Harmon and family of Chesterfield, Virginia; Scott Harmon of Hopewell, Virginia. Memorials to your choice or Veterans Memorial Library, 1600 Veterans Parkway, Lancaster, Texas 75134.

Pickvance Sr.

COL. WILLIAM W., USAF (Ret.) 79. who died Tuesday, September 17, 2002 at his residence in Gainesville, Texas. Funeral services will be held at 2:30 p.m. on Friday, September 20th in the Dannel Funeral Home Chapel. Chaplain Ziegler of the United States Air Force will officiate. Interment will follow at West Hill Cemetery will full military honors.

Dannel Funeral Home
302 S. Walnut
Sherman, Texas 75090
903-893-1171

American Red Cross, Dallas Area Chapter, 4800 Harry Hines Blvd., Dallas, Tx 75235-7717; or a charity of choice.

PIERCE

DAISY, born Aug. 5, 1915 in Joplin, MO, passed away Sept. 18, 2002 in Dallas at the age of 87. She is survived by 4 daughters: Virginia Ledibrand, Sybil Panko, Kathryn Gutierrez and Debby Romero; 1 son; George Beagle; grandchildren; Carrie Molina, Terrell Pierce, Eddie Rouillard, Anthony Rouillard and Danny Caldwell; 14 great-grandchildren. Funeral services will be held at 1:30 PM Monday, Sept. 23 at the Heritage Funeral Home Chapel with Elder Leonard Willis officiating. Interment will follow at Calvary Hill Memorial Park. The family will receive friends from 6:00 PM to 9:00 PM Sunday evening at the funeral home. She is loved very much and will be missed dearly. We love you Mom and Grandma!

HERITAGE FUNERAL HOME
4408 Gaston Ave.
Dallas, TX   214-887-3555

ROWLEY

RITGER

SHIRLEY W. , born September 20, 1922 in Cleveland, Mississippi, the daughter of William Bernard and Virgie Middleton Woodyear, died on September 19, 2002 in Dallas, Texas. She moved to Dallas in 1976 after living in El Dorado, Arkansas for 28 years. In El Dorado, she was an active member of First Baptist Church, the Charity League, and various civic organizations and served as a Girl Scout leader. In Dallas, she was a member of First Baptist Church of Richardson, Town North Women's Club, and Fretz Park Senior Center. She is survived by her husband of 58 years Andrew G. Ritger, Sr., her daughters and sons-in-law Holly and David M. Sudbury, Robin and Thomas T. Milam of Grass Valley, California, her son and daughter-in-law Andrew G. Ritger, Jr. and Elizabeth Branham, five grandchildren, Erin Sudbury and Gregory Sudbury of Dallas, Lila Ritger, Andrew G. Ritger, III, and Charles Ritger of Edmond, Oklahoma. Memorial Service will be held at Cox Chapel of Highland Park United Methodist Church in Dallas on Friday, September 20, 2002 at 3:00pm. Private interment will be at

grandchildre
Robert, Bret
thew, Eli
Bryce; siste
husband R
many other
ews and co
will receive
Friday, Se
2002 from 6-
al services
the chapel
Funeral Ho
day, Septem
at 10:00 A.M

3920 Samue
(214)

SEPULV

GASPAR GU
born on Octo
Nuevo Lar
and to our
passed awa
15, 2002. He
by his loving
wife of 41
Guadalupe
sons; Gaspa
Rosalva, F
wife, Cher
Gustavo and
daughters;
Nannapanen
band, Mural
pita White
Michael. We
ber his keen
mor, his poet
and his pro

Birth Father

Earl F. Beagle
1940 Census Record

Line 75
1940 U.S. Federal Population Census
National Archives
View full citation

Gender: Male   Race: White

Age at Time of Census: 29   Estimated Birth Year: 1911

Birth Location: Missouri Map

Enumeration District: 116-51

Residence: Ward 3, Kansas City, Kaw Township, Jackson, MO Map

Language: English   Marital Status: Married

Relationship to Head: Head

Members in Household

Daisey Beagle
24 yrs, Female

Syble Beagle
2 yrs, Female

Virginia Beagle
5 yrs, Female

George Beagle
3 yrs, Male

Suggested Records for Earl Beagle

1930 Census - 1 record
Earl Beagle, born in MO, around 1911

Historic Newspapers - 2 mentions
Earl Beagle located in MO

ARCHIVES

Search All Archives
Vital Records
Military Records
Living People Search

Cemetery Listings
Census Records
Immigration & Passenger Lists

Newspapers
Yearbooks
Obituaries
Surname Histories

Deaths

St. Joseph Gazette - Page 2C
1/6/1988

Earl Beagle

Earl F. Beagle, (77) 621 N. Ninth St., died Tuesday, Jan. 5, 1988, at a St. Joseph hospital.

Mr. Beagle was born in Stotts City, Mo.

He had worked at the Salvation Army for 40 years and was a retired World War II veteran serving in the Army.

Surviving

a sister,
Georgia Corbin, Camdenton, Mo.

The body has been cremated under the direction of the Heaton-Bowman-Smith and Sidenfaden Chapel. There will be no services held.

did he have T.B.

-No Name

He was born in 1911

Earl Beagle (My 1st Dad)

Foster Care

Verda, born Jeanette Beagle, was placed in the welfare system when she was five months old. There were mitigating circumstances surrounding Jeannette's placement in the welfare system. Daisy Beagle had fallen 30 feet from a trestle above St. Louis Avenue and was struck by a street car going in the opposite direction. She was 27 years old with five children. Daisy was on her way to look for a job when the accident happened. She suffered internal injuries, fractured ribs and lacerations to her face and legs. She stayed in a hospital for about a year, unable to care for her children. Thus, all her four other children were placed in foster care during her stay in the hospital.

During this time, Earl had deserted Daisy when he joined the Army. Having her husband leave her was difficult. Daisy knew he was in the US Army; however, she did not know the means to go about finding him. When Daisy was released from the hospital, she had a decision to make regarding the care of her five children that had been placed in foster care. She knew she was unable to care for the family; however, the four older children wanted to go home with "mama." Daisy realizing the financial difficulty taking care of the five children which included a baby, she chose to let her baby, Jeannette, stay in the children's home (foster care).

The decision to leave her youngest child, Jeanette, was not an easy one. Daisy knew it would be difficult financially to care for the older children. Verda was in the welfare system approximately one year before she was eligible for foster care. In the foster care system after a year she was placed with an affluent Negro couple, Ray and Edwinna Wagner in Newton Kansas. Jeanette thrived in the care of Ray and Edwinna. Although Jeanette was born of a "White" mother and father, there was no problem placing her in their home. In January 1946, Edwinna and Ray had notified the Child Adoption Department in writing that they wanted to adopt. Verda remained with the Wagners until she could be legally adopted.

Adoption

On January 14, 1944, Jeanette Beagle's, birth mother, Daisy Beagle, signed consent to adopt papers, thus releasing Jeanette to the State of Missouri. Jeanette's birth father, Earl Beagle signed consent to adopt on February 28, 1945. Earl Beagle had gone into the U.S. Army in October 1943 and was not available to sign the appropriate paperwork until he was discharged.

IN THE CIRCUIT COURT OF JACKSON COUNTY, MISSOURI,
AT KANSAS CITY,
JUVENILE DIVISION

In re adoption of

JEANNETTE BEAGLE

RAY WAGNER   Petitioners
EDWINNA WAGNER

No.

CONSENT TO ADOPTION OF A CHILD

I declare that I am the mother of _Jeanette Beagle_, a _Fe_male child born _9-27_ 19_42_, and residing in Jackson County, Missouri, and I hereby consent to the adoption of said child by the petitioners in proceedings for such adoption which have been, or will hereafter be, instituted in the Juvenile Division of the Circuit Court of Jackson County, Missouri, at Kansas City, which adoption shall be subject to the approval and direction of said Court or the Judge thereof. I further agree that I shall not hereafter have any right or claim for services, wages, control, custody, or company of said child and that from the date of the decree of adoption said child shall, to all legal intents and purposes, be the child of the person or persons so adopting said child.

* Mrs. Daisy Beagle

STATE OF MISSOURI,
County of Jackson,   ss.

On this................day of........................, 194......, before me, a Notary Public in and for said County and State, personally appeared ...., to me known to be the person described in and who executed the foregoing instrument and acknowledged the same as her free act and deed for the uses and purposes therein mentioned.

IN TESTIMONY WHEREOF, I have hereunto set my hand and affixed my official seal at my office in Kansas City, Jackson County, Missouri, the day and year first above written.

My term expires........................

Witness
Anna B. Clement
_1-14-44_

....
Notary Public in and for said County and State.

On February 26, 1945 Earl Beagle signed the Consent to Adoption of a Child. Jeanette was 2 ½ years old. Earl Beagle had left the family and joined the military. When Earl returned, he signed the consent form.

IN THE CIRCUIT COURT OF JACKSON COUNTY, MISSOURI,
AT KANSAS CITY,
JUVENILE DIVISION

In re adoption of
JEANETTE BEAGLE

RAY O WAGNER
EDWINNA WAGNER

No.

Petitioners

CONSENT TO ADOPTION OF A CHILD

I declare that I am the Husband of the Mother of *Jeanette Beagle*, a Fe.male child born 9-27, 1942, and residing in Jackson County, Missouri, and I hereby consent to the adoption of said child by the petitioners in proceedings for such adoption which have been, or will hereafter be, instituted in the Juvenile Division of the Circuit Court of Jackson County, Missouri, at Kansas City, which adoption shall be subject to the approval and direction of said Court or the Judge thereof. I further agree that I shall not hereafter have any right or claim for services, wages, control, custody, or company of said child and that from the date of the decree of adoption said child shall, to all legal intents and purposes, be the child of the person or persons so adopting said child.

Earl F. Beagle

STATE OF MISSOURI,
County of Jackson, ss.

On this................day of..................., 194......, before me, a Notary Public in and for said County and State, personally appeared ...., to me known to be the person described in and who executed the foregoing instrument and acknowledged the same as her free act and deed for the uses and purposes therein mentioned.

IN TESTIMONY WHEREOF, I have hereunto set my hand and affixed my official seal at my office in Kansas City, Jackson County, Missouri, the day and year first above written.

My term expires................

Witness
Emma B. Clement
Lena Ware
Feb. 26, 1945

....
Notary Public in and for said County and State.

In January 1946, Edwinna Wagner notified the Child Adoption Department, in writing that she had been visiting her mother in Chicago who was very ill. However, she wanted the Department to know that "Verda Ann" had quite a Christmas with her new family. Among the many Christmas gifts was a shiny new tricycle.

On January 13, 1946 Edwinna sent a letter to the Child Adoption Department, Juvenile Court, Kansas City, Missouri in c/o Miss Dear Miss Mary Lou Fenberg. The letter to Miss Fenberg reads:

"Dear Miss Fenberg: I am sorry to have waited so long to write this letter, but I was quite busy during December, and getting ready for the holidays, (our first Christmas with our little Verda Ann), and now I am in Chicago with my mother, who is very, very ill.

Verda Ann had quite a Christmas as she received many things including the tricycle she has wanted so long. She has been doing fine, except a little cold but is over with now, she is growing and as fat as a butter ball. I had the doctor to examine her in November, and he said she was O.K. except a little pus in her urine, but nothing serious.

I would like to know what vaccinations or injections she has had as our school give certain vaccinations ever so often, and last fall were giving...."

Edwinna's seriousness in the letter testifies to the love she has for the child, Verda Ann, was in their home as a foster child. Edwinna and Ray doted on their "only child." You could say they felt that Jeanette was a "God-send" to them.

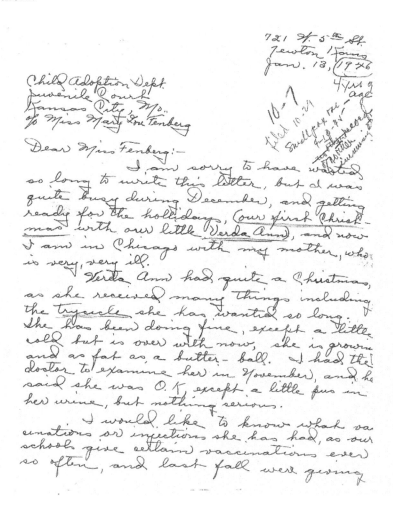

On October 3, 1946 Ray and Edwinna Wagner filed Application Blank for Those Interested in Adopting a Child" in Kansas City, Missouri to adopt Jeanette Beagle. A copy of the application is below.

Ray Oval Wagner and Edwinna W. Cole Wagner had been married nine years at the time they applied for the adoption of Jeanette Beagle. At that time, she had been in foster care status with the Wagners for eight months. They felt that Jeanette was a "perfect" fit for the family.

On October 7, 1946 Ray O. Wagner and Edwinna W. Wagner filed a Petition for Control and Custody of Child. The child, Jeanette Beagle, was in the custody and control of the Jackson County Juvenile Court. On said date the control and custody of Jeanette Beagle was transferred to the petitioners, pending final approval or denial of petition for adoption.

AT KANSAS CITY,

JUVENILE DIVISION

—

PETITION FOR CONTROL AND CUSTODY OF CHILD.

Comes now your petitioners .... RAY O. AND EDWINNA W. WAGNER ....

....and pray the Court for permission to have

the control and custody of .... JEANETTE BEAGLE ....

a child, who is now in the custody and control of .... JACKSON COUNTY JUVENILE COURT

....and that said control and custody of said

child be transferred and surrendered to your petitioners until the petition for the

adoption of said child be finally approved or denied by the Juvenile Court of Jackson

County, Missouri.

Ray O. Wagner

Edwinna W. Wagner

Petitioners.

It is hereby ordered that the control and custody of..... JEANETTE BEAGLE ....

....be in and is hereby transferred to

..... RAY O. AND EDWINNA W. WAGNER ...., petitioners, pending

the final approval or denial of the petition for adoption.

Ray S. Cowan

Judge of the Juvenile Court.

Dated this........7........day of..... October ...., 19 46

E-78887

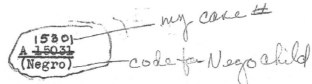

(530)
A 15031
(Negro)

my case #
code for Negro child

Ray Oval Wagner and Edwinna W. Cole Wagner –
              721 West Fifth Street – Newton, Kansas

Child – Jeanette Beagle – female – born September 27, 1942

Mr. Ray Oval Wagner is 45 years of age and his wife is 43. They
have been married for 9 years and have had no children of their
marriage. Mr. and Mrs. Wagner love children and are not able to
have them. For that reason, they are petitioning for the adoption
of the child who has been in their home for the past 8 months as
they feel certain she fits perfectly into their family and has a
definite place in the home.

Mr. Wagner is a train porter for the Santa Fe Railway. He has
an income of $250.00 a month and personal property of $1,500.00.
Mr. Wagner has life insurance of $4,000.00 and owns his home
which is valued at $4,500.00.

Mr. and Mrs. Wagner are members of the Methodist Church and will
rear their child in this faith. They plan a college education for
their daughter.

This placement was made by the ~~Adoption~~ Probation Department.

_____

References:

Attached to this case are letters of reference submitted by Mr.
and Mrs. Wagner. Also attached is a report from their physician
who states that the child is developing normally and is receiving
excellent care and training.

Agent's report:

The department recommends that this adoption be allowed.

                                    Mary Lou Ferberg
                                             Agent

_____

6-5-47

Approved:

                    Richmond B. Dunvan
                         Guardian ad Litem

Placed: October 7, 1946
In home: 8 months

It is interesting to note that the Kansas Children's Home and Service League thoroughly conducted the study of the Wagner home. On March 16, 1946 Miss Ruth V. Clark notified the Wagners in writing that the application for a child had been completely approved. That letter is below followed by another letter from the children's home dated October 8, 1946. Interesting enough the "Worker believes that this is a Negro family, far above average cultural standards and interests." One wonders where we cross the line from believing it is a Negro family to knowing it is a Negro family that is far above average cultural standards and interest.

All roads lead to the fact that the State of Kansas was going to do whatever necessary to make sure "Jeanette" ended up in the Wagner family as "Verda."

In the Circuit Court of Jackson County, Missouri, at Kansas City

JUVENILE DIVISION

In re adoption of

JEANETTE BEAGLE

RAY O. WAGNER

EDWINNA W. WAGNER

Petitioners.

No.

PETITION FOR PERMISSION TO ADOPT A CHILD

Now comes......RAY O. WAGNER...................... and ...EDWINNA W. WAGERN............

his wife, and petition the Court for permission to adopt as their child.....JEANETTE BEAGLE.....

.....FEMALE.........child born on the......27....day of.........September............, 1946, and

residing in Jackson County, Missouri.

Petitioners say that they reside together as husband and wife at......Newton..........

in the State of.............Kansas.............., that they are of good moral character; that they have a

comfortable home in a desirable neighborhood, that they have an income in excess of....$200..........per

month and that they are able to properly care for, maintain and educate said child and give it proper

moral and religious training.

That the xxxxxxxxxxxxxxxxxxxxxxxxxxxxxxxxxxxxxparents of said child give written consent to this adoption; said consents being attached hereto and made a part hereof.

Petitioners request that guardian ad litem be appointed herein, and that the name of said child be

changed to....VERDA ANN WAGNER...................

WHEREFORE, Petitioners pray the court to enter a decree ordering that from the date thereof

said child shall, to all legal intents and purposes, be the child of the petitioners, and that the name of the

said child be changed to..VERDA ANN WAGNER...........................

Signed   *Ray O. Wagner*
Edwinna W. Wagner   Oct. 7, 46

STATE OF MISSOURI } ss.
COUNTY OF JACKSON }

Before me, a Notary Public duly commissioned and qualified personally appeared the above petitioners....Ray O. Wagner............ and Edwinna W. Wagner............ whom being duly sworn on their oath states they have read the above and foregoing petition, have signed the same and that the facts therein are true according to their best knowledge and belief.

Mary Lou Finley
Notary Public in and for the Said County and State

Subscribed and sworn to before me this 7 day of......October............ 19 46. My commission will expire............April 11, 1950

After adoption, October 13, 1946 The Wagners notified in Child Adoption Department that Verda Ann was adjusting very well. The following is letter Edwinna Sent to Mrs. Fenberg.

"721 W. 5th St.

Newton, Kansas

October 13, 1946

Mrs. Mary Lou Fenberg, Supervisor

Child Adoption Unit

Juvenile Court Bldg.

Dear Mrs. Fenberg: On leaving the court building, then getting in the taxi, Verda Ann quieted down and became interested in the taxi and various objects on the streets, and I had no trouble from then on. She became friendly and played with my husband later at my sister-in-laws (sic); and is very fond of him now, in fact he is reading the funny paper to her now.

She is doing fine, having had only two period (sic) of homesickness, where she cried to go back to her other mama and daddy (sic) and wanted her other play things. But we are hoping she will forget in time, although she has such a wonderful memory, in fact we have found her to have a very brilliant mind in comparison to a child of five or six. She is sweet and we love her very much already.

She has played with Bobby almost every day this week.

I am enclosing the letter you asked for."

Knowing that follow-up contact was necessary in the adoption process, Mrs. Ray Wagner notified the Child Adoption Department, in writing, to update status on how Verda Ann was adjusting. The following are contents of letter:

```
                              January 20, 1947



        Mrs. Ray O. Wagner
        721 West 5th Street
        Newton
        Kansas

        Dear Mrs. Wagner:

                        Our records show that Verda Ann
        was given small pox vaccination on April 10, 1945,
        and that she has had no other immunizations.

                        We are so delighted that the little
        girl is developing so well and that you are so
        happy with her.

                        Very truly yours


                        (Mrs.) Myrtle W. Tabot
```

National Association for the Advancement of Colored People

NEWTON KANSAS BRANCH

Newton, Kansas

721 N. 5th St.
Newton, Kans.
Oct. 13, 1946

Mrs. Mary Lou Fenberg
Supervisor
Child Adoption Dept.
Juvenile Court Bldg.

Dear Mrs. Fenberg:—

On leaving the court building, then getting in the taxi, Verda Ann quieted down and became interested in the taxi and various objects on the streets, and I had no trouble from then on. She became friendly and played with my husband later at my sister-in-law's, and is very fond of him now, in fact he is reading the funny paper to her now.

She is doing fine, having had only two periods of homesickness, where she cried to go back to her other mama and dady, and wanted her other play things. But we are hoping she will forget in time, although she has such a wonderful memory, in fact we have found her to have a very brilliant mind, in comparison to a child of five or six. She is sweet and we love her very much already.

She has played with Bobby almost every day this week.

I am enclosing the letter you asked for.

Respectfully, yours

"721 W. 5th St.
Newton, Kansas
April 25, 1947

Child Adoption Dept
Juvenile Court Bldg.
Kansas City, Mo.
c/o Mrs. Myrtle Tabot

Dear Mrs. Tabot

　　Since we were getting along so well I had forgotten that I should make another report before the seven month period is ended. So I am happy to report that our little girl, Verda Ann, is doing fine.

　　However, some time ago she had quite a spell of vomiting, etc., but after having two different doctors, one a child specialist, they found nothing serious wrong after various tests were taken. Possibly a little nervous condition due to the death of my mother. I was told to watch her kidneys as they showed albumen content. So after taking some medicine she is doing fine at present.

　　It has been some time since she mentioned her "other home," and the last time I remember her mentioning it, it was with very little emphasis. That it was unimportant compared to previous remarks.

　　She is looking forward to what she believes will be the happiest moment in her life, the day she will begin, or rather start in kindergarden (sic).

　　She can count to fifteen knows some of her A.B.C's and can make some of them but can recognize most of them, can spell Verda Ann, knows her telephone number and street number, town, etc. and any number of things that I don't recall just now.

　　So we are quite proud of her.

　　　　　　　　　　Sincerely

　　　　　　　　　　Mrs. Ray Wagner

721 W. 5th St.
Newton, Kans.
April 25th, 1947

Child Adoption Dept.
Juvenile Court Bldg.
Kansas City, Mo.
℅ Mrs. Myrtle Tabot.

Dear Mrs. Tabot:—

Since we were getting along so well, I had forgotten that I should make another report before the seven month period is ended. So I am happy to report that our little girl, Verda Ann, is doing fine.

However, some time ago she had quite a spell of vomiting, etc., but after

II

having two different doctors, one a child specialist, they found nothing serious wrong, after various tests were taken. Possibly a little nervous condition due to the death of my mother. I was told to watch her kidney as they showed albumen content. So after taking some medicine she is doing fine at present.

It has been some time since she mentioned her "other home"; and the last time I remember her mentioning it, it was with very little emphasis. That it was unimportant compared to previous remarks.

She is looking foward

III

to what she believes will be the happiest moment in her life, the day she will began, or rather start in kindergarden.

She can count to fifteen, knows some of her A. B. C's, and can make some of them, but can recognize most of them, can spell Verda Ann, knows her telephone number and street number, town etc.. And any number of things that I don't recall just now.

So we are quite proud of her.

Sincerely
Mrs. Ray Wagner

721 West 5th St.
Newton Kansas
May 26th, 1947

Adoption Department
1305 Locust St.
Kansas City, 6 Missouri

Dear Mrs. Talbot:—

    We have now had little Verda Ann in our home for seven months. We have watched her grow and progress, and she has taken a definite place in our home and our hearts, as we feel she is our own child and love her as our own. We wish to secure the final papers on her so she will indeed be our own child.

    We both feel we cannot ever thank you enough for your help, in filling this important spot in our lives, by bringing us together. So, it is our hope that we may secure the final papers of adoption as soon as possible.

Respectfully yours,
Edwinna Wagner
Ray O. Wagner

P.S.

    As Verda Ann was exposed to whooping cough a couple of weeks ago, but up to date has showed no signs of taking the desease, I am wondering if she has already had it and what other childs desease she has had, or would you have a record of any. If you have, I would appreciate very much your letting me know about this. Thanking you for your trouble.

Sincerely,
Mrs. Ray O. Wagner

On May 28, 1947 Dr. Robert W. Myers of The Bethel Clinic notified the Adoption Department that Verda Ann was developing normally both mentally and physically.

"The Bethel Clinic
210 South Pine Street
Newton, Kansas

May 28, 1947

Adoption Department
1305 Locust Street
Kansas City 6, Missouri

Dear Sir:

In compliance with your instructions to foster parents, we are writing to you concerning Verda Ann Wagner who is being adopted by R.A. Wagner of 721 W. 5th, Newton, Kansas. She was seen by Dr. J.B. Nanninga of this clinic as well as myself and we feel that this child is developing normally both mentally and physically and is extremely fortunate to have the good care which she is receiving. I saw this child in a school round-up of the pre-school children in preparation to entrance into kindergarten. She is a very polite and well mannered child and answers questions intelligently.

If there is any further questions concerning her, please feel free to write us.
Sincerely

Robert W. Myers, M.D.

On June 3, 1947, the Wagners received the long-awaited news; the State was ready to finalize the adoption.

"June 5, 1947

Mrs. Ray O. Wagner

721 West Fifth Street

Newton

Kansas

Dear Mrs. Wagner:

We will be happy to complete your adoption of Verda Ann into your family. We are very happy that she has progressed so nicely and that you are so happy with her.

Verda Ann has had two whooping cough shots, been vaccinated against smallpox, and has had the measles. She has had no illness other than that.

As soon as we have completed this case and have the final papers for you, we shall mail them.

Very truly yours

_____

(Mrs.) Myrtle W. Talbot"

Note: The original was not signed by Mrs. Talbot

As you walk with Verda Ann through her early life, it is interesting to note that the State of Missouri issued two birth certificates on her—one as Jeanette Beagle and the other Verda Ann Wagner. The certified copy of birth record depicting the Wagners as birth parents was certified at the age of 3 on the 14th day of July 1947.

Jeanette Beagle was born of White parents, Earl and Daisy Beagle, thus Jeannette is a White child. When Ray an Edwinna Wagner were issued a certified copy of birth record for Verda Ann Wagner, the race had been changed to Negro. (See copy below.)

In the Circuit Court of Jackson County, Missouri, at Kansas City:

JUVENILE DIVISION

In re adoption of   Jeanette Beagle

Ray O. Wagner and
Edwinna W. Wagner   No. A.15301

                                        Petitioners

NOW, on this   5th   day of   June   19 47 , the petition of

Ray O. Wagner and Edwinna W. Wagner   for

the adoption of   Jeanette Beagle   coming on to be heard and

the report of   Richard B. Kirwan   guardian ad litem for said child

in these proceedings, having been made herein, the said   Jeanette Beagle

minor, being present in person and by said guardian ad litem, and the evidence being heard, and

the court being fully advised finds:

That said   Jeanette Beagle   is a minor, under the age of 12 years

and resides in Jackson County, Missouri, born September 27th, 1942.

The court further finds   that both natural parents of said minor child, give
written consent to this adoption and
are   that said petition for adoption and the parental consent to such adoption
is in legal form and that the report of said guardian ad litem is favorable to said adoption. The Court
is satisfied that the persons petitioning to adopt said child are of good character and of sufficient
ability to properly care for, maintain and educate such child, and that the welfare of such child will be
promoted by sustaining said petition for adoption; and that it is fit and proper that such adoption
should be made.

WHEREFORE, it is adjudged, ordered and decreed, that from the date of this decree, said child

shall, to and for all legal intents and purposes become and be the child of Ray O. Wagner and

Edwinna W. Wagner   and that the name of said child shall

be changed to Verda Ann Wagner.

It is further adjudged, ordered and decreed that the natural parents of said child shall, in no wise
hereafter have any right or claim to or for the services, wages, control, custody or company of said child.

STATE OF MISSOURI, }
County of Jackson,   } ss.   THOMAS J. GILL
                                I, BERNARD OREANNERY, Clerk of the Circuit

6021

KANSAS CITY, MISSOURI
DEPARTMENT OF HEALTH
Bureau of Vital Statistics

CERTIFIED COPY OF BIRTH RECORD

District No. 149   Primary Registration District No. 1002   Registrar's No. AL 5

OF BIRTH:	2. USUAL RESIDENCE OF MOTHER:
ty Jackson	(a) State Kansas (b) County Harvey
or town Kansas City	
(If outside city or town limits, write "RURAL" and name of township)	(c) City or town Newton
e of hospital or institution:	(If outside city, or town limits write "rural" and name of tav
(If not in hospital or institution, write street number or location)	
's stay before delivery:	(d) Street No. 721 W. 5th St.
pital or institution In this community	(If rural, give location)
(Specify whether years, months, or days)	

4. Date of birth September 27, 19
(Month)   (Day)

ame of child Verda Ann Wagner

Female	6. Twin or triplet	If so—born 1st, 2d, or 3d	7. Number months pregnancy (9)	8. Is mother married? Y

FATHER OF CHILD	MOTHER OF CHILD
ame Ray Oval Wagner	15. Full maiden name Edwinna Cole
or race Negro 11. Age at time of this birth 41 yrs.	16. Color or race Negro 17. Age at time of this birth
lace Chelsea Oklahoma	18. Birthplace Perry Oklahom
(City, town, or county) (State or foreign country)	(City, town, or county) (State or foreign
Occupation Railroad Porter	19. Usual occupation Housewife
try or business	20. Industry or business
en born to this mother: (Not including this child.)	22. Mother's mailing address for registration notice:
any other children of this mother are now living? 0	721 W. 5th St.
any other children were born alive but are now dead? 0	Newton, Kansas
any children were born dead? 0	

eby certify that I attended the birth of this child who was born alive at the hour of 11:25 P. on the date above stated and that the in
en was furnished by   related to this child as

received by local registrar 10/9/42	Attendant's own signature Druery R. Thorn
trar's own signature M. M. Crowe	M. D., D. O., midwife, or other M. D. Date signed 10/
on which given name added by	Address Kansas City, Missouri
Registrar	

Missouri,
Kansas City

ereby certify that the above is a true and correct copy of the certificate of birth of Verda Ann Wagner
the office of Vital Statistics of Kansas City, Missouri; that the above certificate is filed in said office and is a part of the
of the Bureau of Vital Statistics of Kansas City, Missouri.

Witness my hand as Director of Health, Kansas City, Missouri this 14th

day of July, 19 47

Hugh L. Dwyer, M.D.
DIRECTOR OF HEALTH

Registrar.

50c

O—0000

Transracial Adoption

Had Verda's race remained as White on the Certified Copy of Birth Record that was provided to the Wagners, Verda's adoption would have been "officially" considered a transracial adoption. At that time, according to Verda, she felt the State of Missouri did not want "non White" children in their child welfare agencies because it was a "slave" and "segregated" State. When the State of Missouri gave permission for a Negro couple to adopt Verda, she was taken out of her birth race; thus a transracial adoption. One wonders if there were officials who assumed Verda was a "light skinned" Negro child because a Negro couple wanted to adopt her. Verda felt blessed to have been adopted by a family who was able to love her and provide the amenities required as she was growing up.

In an article, *Facts and Consequences of Inappropriate and Transracial Adoptions,"* Item 3 from the subheading, "Transracial Adoption.(Black Children vs. White Children) in the article are quoted.

"Social workers often were urgent to arrange inappropriate adoptions so the state could get federal BONUS money. The federal government gave states federal money for each adoption from foster care that was approved thus the "MATCHING (sic) UP" of races and cultures DID NOT occur. Transracial adoptions were done as quickly as possible to just "GET RID OF" or "DISPOSED OF QUICKLY", children who they thought were "NON WHITE"

According to Verda: 1). RACISM did not allow me to have full inclusion of my "WHITE" world and culture. 2). Negro families were sought out to adopt children with "Curly Hair" because the State of MISSOURI "ASSUMED" they were of Negro race. 3) Foster Parents and Adoptive Parents were to be of "LIGHT COMPLEXION" so the "Light SKINNED or white child would not notice too great of a change in their environment or racial identity. 4) I was denied full access of possible opportunities for employment, such as owning a "MAJOR" business, as one of my siblings did. 5). Educational scholarships and grants were never available to me as a NEGRO child as they were to white kids. Bethel College, in Newton Kansas, where I grew up, never offered any kind of financial aid to "BLACK" students. 6). Inappropriate adoptions can lead to psychological and emotional distress.

Verda recommends that emotional injury (emotional distress or mental anguish) should be awarded for letting an inappropriate adoption happen to a "white" child. Further, she feels that punitive damages should be awarded from the State of Missouri because as a victim of inappropriate adoption, personal confusion will always exist from not knowing who Jeanette Beagle (Verda's birth name) really would/could have been.

By the time Verda found out that she was born in a White family it was too late to ascertain from those who made the birth "race" change why such action was taken. As the title depicts, Seventy Years of Blackness, Verda did not know until age 70 that she was born to White parents.

Several letters pertaining to the interest in adopting Jeanette and adoption papers certifying same were reviewed by Verda. There is another letter of interest from the Juvenile Court in Kansas City MO dated September 20, 1946. The letter is addressed to Mr. and Mrs. Donald Kern. The Kerns knew the Wagners and also knew that "Jeanette Beagle" was living with the Wagners. A copy of the letter is quoted below. Note in paragraph 2 of the letter, "We are wondering if she is still interested, as we have a light skinned little girl, now five years old, whom we feel might fit into their home." Of interest is the fact that the child is referred to as a "light skinned little girl."

JUVENILE COURT
KANSAS CITY 6. MO.
1305 LOCUST STREET

RAY G. COWAN,
JUDGE

September 20, 1946

ADOPTION DEPARTMENT
MARY LOU FENBERG
SUPERVISOR

Mr. and Mrs. Donald E. Kern
900 West 12th St., R. R. 1
Newton, Kansas

Dear Mr. and Mrs. Kern:

When you were in our office for your personal interview,
Mrs. Kern mentioned a relative who would be interested in
the adoption of a child.

We are wondering if she is still interested, as we have a
light skinned little girl, now five years old, whom we feel
might fit into their home. May we hear from you in regard
to this matter at your earliest possible convenience.

We imagine that Bobby Joe is in school by this time and are
anxious to hear from you concerning his adjustment in your
home.

My kindest personal regards to both of you.

Very truly yours,

Mary Lou Fenberg

(Mrs.) Mary Lou Fenberg
Supervisor

MLF:md

FOUNDED   1893

Kansas Children's Home and Service League

Wichita 12, Kansas
March 15, 1946

Mr. and Mrs. Ray O. Wagner
721 West 5th
Newton, Kansas

Dear Mr. and Mrs. Wagner:

We are glad to tell you that your application for a child has been completely approved.

Because children are so different and because we must find a home that will be what each child needs, it may be some time before your home is used. As soon as we are able to use your home for a particular child we will get in touch with you.

Very truly yours,

Miss Marjorie Foulke,
State Case Supervisor

By (Miss) Ruth V. Clark,
Wichita Case Supervisor

RVC:HR

FOUNDED 1893

Kansas Children's Home and Service League

October 8, 1946

Mrs. Mary Lou Fenberg, Supervisor
Adoption Dep't, Juvenile Court
1305 Locust Street
Kansas City, Missouri

Re: Ray & Edwina Wagner
    Newton, Kansas

Dear Mr. Fenberg:

Your letter regarding the Ray Wagner home study, has been received. The Wagner application was received on 10-2-45. The medical reports were approved and a home study approved on March 15, 1946.

The worker, who made the study of this home, has recorded the following evaluation:

Worker believes that this is a negro family, far above average cultural standards and interests. They are acknowledged leaders in their community and apparently have sound ideas on the racial situation and other things that might affect a colored child's adjustment to the community. They have out-going personalities which would tend to make a child's life enjoyable. The family is assured of sufficient income to offer economic stability to a child. Worker feels, that because of their age the first few months of adjustment might be more difficult than the family realizes, but believes that the family, because of their personalities, could easily make this adjustment. Worker would recommend that the family be considered as an adoptive home for a child of around two years of age. Worker feels that, either a rather light child or one of a dark brown, rather than black coloring, would fit best in this home.

If we can be of any other service to you, please feel free to write me.

Very truly yours,

(Miss) Helen Griffin, Supervisor
Foster Home Department

HG:rr

Transracial Adoption Example

The Kerns, also of Newton, Kansas, adopted a little boy. Verda knows the boy they adopted and as adults they still keep in touch. The young man ended up in the Kerns home as his second adopted family. The boy's mother is White. He was in foster care and later adopted by a White family. The same caseworker, Ms. Fenberg, was assigned the case. Below is quoted an article that appeared in a Kansas City newspaper.

" 'White' Baby Changed to Negro; Seek New Parents"

The tragedy of racial segregation in America is being felt in a white Southside home. And the real victim is a 4 ½ year old boy who will suffer psychologically and perhaps economically.

When the youngster was an infant, he was taken to the juvenile court for adoption by his mother. In giving the history of the birth, the mother who was white, told the authorities that the father also was white.

But time has told another story.

Have Comfortable Home

The child was adopted by a well-to-do family out South.

When the boy was about a year old, his foster parents noticed a tendency toward Negroid features but their love for the child was so great that they could not bear to part with the youngster and did nothing about it.

But now, at the age of four, the child has been found to be without a doubt a Negro.

The adoptive parents still do not want to give up the child, but because of segregated pattern in Missouri, they find it necessary. The child cannot attend the white school in the Southside neighborhood because of Missouri law. His playmates tease him because of his hair.

The boy, being sensitive as well as attractive, intelligent and alert, senses that something is amiss but he does not know what it is.

Something must be done and quickly.

Therefore, Miss Mary Lou Fenberg of the juvenile court is trying to find a Negro family to adopt the child.

Miss Fenberg and other authorities think it better for the psychological reaction of the child that the new foster parents both be of light complexion. Thus, the child will not notice too great a change of his environment.

Miss Fenberg is anxious that the new parents have a comfortable home and that they will be capable of giving the youngster all the love and care that he has been getting from his white foster parents.

The court has been unable so far to contact the child's real mother to get definite information on the boy's racial identity.

Persons interested in the little boy, can reach Miss Fenberg through whom the adoption will be made, ay the Jackson County Parental home, 1305 Locust St., Ha. 6767."

Kansas City Newspaper early also had 46 printed this article about another child

thus K.C. MO. was trying to get rid of "Welfare" kids any way they could for any reason

Phone HArrison 6767-6768-6769

MARY LOU FENBERG
Supervisor
CHILD ADOPTION DEPARTMENT
JUVENILE COURT

JUVENILE COURT BLDG.
1305 LOCUST STREET

KANSAS CITY, MO.

'White' Baby Changes To Negro; Seek New Parents

The tragedy of racial segregation in America is being felt in a white Southside home. And the real victim is a 4½-year-old boy who will suffer psychologically and perhaps economically.

When the youngster was an infant, he was taken to the juvenile court for adoption by his mother. In giving the history of the birth, the mother who was white, told the authorities that the father also was white.

But time has told another story.

Have Comfortable Home

The child was adopted by a well-to-do family out South.

When the boy was about a year old, his foster parents noticed a tendency toward Negroid features but their love for the child was so great that they could not bear to part with the youngster and did nothing about it.

But now, at the age of four, the child has been found to be without a doubt a Negro.

The adopted parents still do not want to give up the child, but because of the segregated pattern in Missouri, they find it necessary. The child cannot attend the white school in the Southside neighborhood because of Missouri law. His playmates tease him about his hair.

The boy, being sensitive as well as attractive, intelligent and alert, senses that something is amiss but he does not know what it is.

Something must be done, and quickly.

Therefore, Miss Mary Lou Fenberg of the juvenile court is trying to find a Negro family to adopt the child.

Miss Fenberg and other authorities think it better, for the psychological reaction of the child, that the new foster parents both be of light complexion. Thus, the child will not notice too great a change in his environment.

Adopt Child

Miss Fenberg is anxious that the new parents have a comfortable home and that they will be capable of giving the youngster all the love and care that he has been getting from his white foster parents.

The court has been unable so far to contact the child's real mother to get definite information on the boy's racial identity.

Persons interested in the little boy can reach Miss Fenberg through whom the adoption will be made, at the Jackson County Parental home, 1305 Locust St., Ha. 6767.

Timeline   People &   Adoption Studies/   Topics in   Further   Document   Site
            Organizations   Adoption Science   Adoption History Reading   Archives   Index

Matching

Jeanette Bates, a Chicago attorney, with her
adopted children, Katherine and Edward,
who looked like each other and their
adoptive mother, 1917

Only one percent of all
adoptions in 1987 were
transracial adoptions

Jim Crow Laws

Desegre

Desegregation efforts
reached their peak in
the late 1960 - and early
1970

During much of the twentieth century, matching was the philosophy that governed non-relative adoption. Its goal was to make families socially that would "match" families made naturally. Matching required that adoptive parents be married heterosexual couples who looked, felt, and behaved as if they had, by themselves, conceived other people's children. What this meant in practice was that physical resemblance, intellectual similarity, and racial and religious continuity between parents and children were preferred goals in adoptive families. Matching was the technique that could inject naturalness and realness into a family form stigmatized as artificial and less real than the "real thing." Matching stood for safety and security. Difference spelled trouble.

Under the matching paradigm, one family was substituted for another so carefully, systematically, and completely that the old family was replaced, rendered invisible and unnecessary. This was not usually the case before the twentieth century. Children who were placed did not lose contact with their natal kin, even in the case of very young children placed permanently for adoption. The only matching required by early adoption laws was matching by religion, and these laws were frequently disregarded by child-savers, such as Charles Loring Brace, who preferred matching children with the (Protestant) religion of the placing organization, rather than that of (Catholic) natal kin. In the nineteenth century, many adoptions involved sharing children rather than giving them away.

In contrast, matching was an optimistic, arrogant, and historically novel objective that suggested that a social operation could and should approximate nature by copying it. Between 1920 and 1970, matching was popular, especially among infertile couples who sought to adopt because they were unable to conceive children of their "own." By midcentury, infertility had become an unquestioned qualification for adoption. This reinforced the notion that matching compensated for reproductive failure by promising relationships that could pass for the exclusive, authentic, and permanent bonds of kinship that were only natural.

Matching confronted the central problem of modern adoption. It attempted to create kinship without blood in the face of an enduring equivalence between blood and belonging. The results were paradoxical. Matching reinforced the notion that blood was thicker than water, the very ideology that made adoption inferior, while seeking to equalize and dignify it.

The naturalness of matching still has ardent defenders today, especially with regard to race. Since 1970, however, its dominance has been criticized by movements opposing confidentiality and sealed records. Transracial adoptions and international adoptions also challenge matching by celebrating families deliberately and visibly formed across lines of race, ethnicity, and nation. Open adoption arrangements undercut matching too. They acknowledge an obvious truth that matching concealed: it is possible to have more than one mother, one father, one family.

Document Excerpts

- *Purinton v. Jamrock*, 1907

- W.H. Slingerland, *Child-Placing in Families*, 1919

- *Matter of Vardinakis*, 1936

- Sample Letter to Families Applying for Infants Where the Woman is Over 40 Years of Age, early 1940s

- Placing Children of Unknown Background and the Problem of Matching, 1951

- *Petition of Goldman*, 1954

- Justine Wise Polier, "A Memorandum Concerning Child Adoption Across Religions Lines," 1955

- Sheldon C. Reed, "Skin Color," 1955

- Discussion of the Role of Anthropology in Transracial Adoptions, 1956

- Justine Wise Polier, "Attitudes and Contradictions in Our Culture," 1960

- Muriel McCrea, "The Mix-Match Controversy," 1967

  Further reading about Matching

Transracial Adoption:

The Pros and Cons and the Parents' Perspective

Andrew Morrison

Harvard BlackLetter Law Journal

Vol. 20, 2004
though the IEAP shows Congress' intent to support TRA, it has had a minimal effect because it does not reach private adoption agencies and still allows race to be used as one of many factors in placement decisions by federally funded agencies.
[69]
State legislatures have a long history of regulating segregation in the family.
[70]
For example, in the past, Louisiana and Texas explicitly prohibited TRA and South Carolina prohibited a mixed race family from adopting.
[71]
Two states, Kentucky and Missouri, allowed adoptive parents to return an adopted child if
the child grew up to resemble a person of a different race than that of the parents; Kentucky still maintains such a law.
[7]

2-1-2015

Personal Note/Information

Facts

1. Adoption documented dated 1-24-14 states that both BIOLOGICAL parents are DAISY BEAGLE PIERCE (Death September 18, 2002) and EARL BEAGLE. (Death January 5, 1988)

2. ADOPTION SEARCH REPORT TO THE JACKSON COUNTY FAMILY COURT states:

   ADOPTEE VERDA WAGNER BYRD File # 15301 D.O.B. 09-27-1942

   BIRTH MOTHER: DAISY BEAGLE PIERCE……BIRTH FATHER: EARL BEAGLE

   DEPARTMENT OF HEALTH…..Bureau of Vital Statistics……CERTIFIED COPY OF BIRTH RECORD….says:

   FATHER OF CHILD   MOTHER OF CHILD

   #9 Full name   Ray Oval Wagner   #15 Full Maiden name   Edwinna Cole

   State of Missouri

   City of Kansas City

   I hereby certify that the above is a true and correct copy of the certificate of birth of Verda Ann Wagner filed in the office of Vital STATISTICS OF Kansas City, Missouri; that the above certificate is filed in said office and is a part of the permanent records of the Bureau of Vital Statistics of Kansas City, Missouri   July 14, 1947

   QUESTION
   HOW CAN TWO DIFFERENT WOMEN HAVE THE SAME CHILD??????

   BIRTH MOTHER*****************DAISY BEAGLE ****RACE……. WHITE

   MOTHER OF CHILD************ EDWINNA Cole****RACE………NEGRO

   HOW CAN TWO DIFFERENT MEN BE THE SAME FATHER?????

   BIRTH FATHER******************EARL BEAGLE*********RACE****WHITE

   FATHER OF CHILD***************RAY OVAL WAGNER****RACE****NEGRO

   *******THE CERTIFIED COPY OF BIRTH RECORD IS UNTRUE******The "NAME" of Ray Oval Wagner, father of child and "NAME" of Edwinna Cole, mother of child does not match birth parents name thus the STATE of MISSOURI "LIED" on a CERTIFIED BIRTH RECORD DOCUMENTATION.

FACTS AND CONSEQUENCES OF:
INAPPROPRIATE and TRANSRACIAL Adoptions

1. **The State of Missouri did not want "NON WHITE" children in their child welfare agencies because it being a "SLAVE" and "SEGREGATED" state they "ASSUMED" all others were of the NEGRO RACE.**

2. **My adoption documents (which are attached/enclosed) state both of my natural/biological parents were WHITE but the state let a NEGRO couple adopt me, thus I was TAKEN OUT OF MY BIRTH RACE and became a TRANSRACIAL adoptee. There was no verbal or written document saying this action was agreed upon. THE STATE OF MISSOURI "ASSUMED" I was a "light skinned' negro child because a NEGRO couple wanted to adopt me. (Enclosed document dated September 20,1946)**

Transracial Adoption   (Black children vs White children)

The issue of transracial adoption (adoption of children who are not the same race as the adoptive parents) has come under close scrutiny by courts, legislatures, and the public. Americans are sharply divided on this issue. Is it a positive way to create stable families for needy children and well-meaning adults? Or is it an insidious means of co-opting members of racial minorities and confusing their sense of identity?

In 1972, when the number of African American children adopted annually by white families rose to fifteen thousand, the National Association of Black Social Workers (NABSW) issued its opinion on the subject. Igniting a furious national debate that continued in the mid-1990s, the association equated transracial adoption with cultural Genocide for African Americans.

The NABSW and other minority groups opposed to the adoption of African American children by whites claim that the children are deprived of a true appreciation and understanding of their culture. Their childhood is skewed toward white values and assimilation. Without a sense of racial identity and pride, these children cannot truly belong to the African American community; yet, by the same token, racism prevents their full inclusion in the white world.

Despite these arguments, some African Americans applaud the unconditional love and permanence offered by transracial adoptions. Transracial adoption supporters argue that it is much worse to grow up without any family at all than to be placed with parents of a different race. Because a disproportionate number of African American children are placed in foster care, mixed-race adoptions may be necessary to ensure permanent homes for some African American children. Transracial adoption may also be viewed as an opportunity to achieve Integration on the most basic level.

Controversies involving transracial adoption soon found their way to the courts. In 1992, the Minnesota Supreme Court upheld a district court's order to transfer a three-year-old African American girl from her suburban Minneapolis foster home to her maternal grandparents' home in Virginia (*In re Welfare of D. L.*, 486 N.W.2d 375 [Minn. 1992]). Referred to as Baby D in court records, the child had been raised since birth by white foster parents who had been married for twenty-four years and had already raised three grown children. Baby D's birth mother placed her in foster care almost immediately after delivery and had not seen the child since. When no relatives could be found to claim the child, the foster parents decided to adopt the girl, whom they had grown to love.

3. Social workers often were urged to arrange inappropriate adoptions so the state could get federal BONUS money. The federal government gave states federal money for each adoption from foster care that was approved thus the "MATCHING UP" of races and cultures DID NOT occur. Transracial adoptions were done as quickly as possible to just "GET RID OF" or "DISPOSED OF QUICKLY", children who they thought were "NON WHITE" (Enclosed article "White" baby Changes to Negro; seek New Parents)

    ******HOW DO BABIES CHANGE FROM ONE RACE TO ANOTHER?********

4. RACISM did not allow me to have full inclusion of my "WHITE" world and culture.

5. Negro families were sought out to adopt children with "Curly Hair" because the State of MISSOURI "ASSUMED" they were of the NEGRO race. (Enclosed article about "White" baby)

6. Foster Parents and Adoptive Parents were to be of "LIGHT COMPLEXION" so the "Light SKINNED" or white child would not notice too great of a change in their environment or racial identity.

7. I was denied full access of possible opportunities for employment, such as owning a "MAJOR" business, as one of my sibling did.

8. Educational scholarships and grants were never available to me as a NEGRO child as they were to white kids. Bethel College, in Newton Kansas, where I grew up, never offered any kind of financial aid to "BLACK" students

9. Inappropriate adoptions can lead to psychologically and emotional distress.

EMOTIONAL INJURY (EMOTIONAL DISTRESS OR MENTAL ANGUISH) SHOULD BE AWARDED FOR LETTING AN INAPPROPRIATE ADOPTION HAPPEN TO A "WHITE" CHILD (all documents were not checked for race)
PUNITIVE DAMAGES FROM THE STATE OF MISSOURI SHOULD BE AWARDED BECAUSE AS A VICTIM OF INAPPROPRIATE ADOPTION: PERSONAL CONFUSION WILL ALWAYS EXIST FROM NOT KNOWING WHO JEANETTE BEAGLE (my birth name) REALLY WOULD/COULD HAVE BEEN

The Wagners

Ray and Edwinna Johnson Wagner were residing in Newton, Kansas when they adopted Jeannette Beagle. Ray Wagner was born August 24, 1901 **in Oklahoma**; his wife, Edwinnia Johnson Wagner was born July 13, 1903 **in Oklahoma**. In earlier years, they moved to Newton, Kansas. Newton, Kansas is located twenty minutes north of Wichita, Kansas. When you drive through the heart of the community, you see a City full of pride for its past.

Ray Oval Wagner was born in Chelsea, Oklahoma on August 24, 1901. He was one of six children. He lived in Oklahoma for a short time, moving to Newton, Kansas where he graduated grade school. He went to prep school and high school in Chicago, Illinois; graduating in 1929. Ray took a four-year pre-legal course at the Lewis Institute in Chicago but was forced to leave school because of the depression after which he commenced working for the Franklin Automobile Company in Chicago. He returned to Newton, Kansas in 1934 at which time he began his career working for the Atchison, Topeka and Santa Fe Railroad.

Ray Wagner had been married prior to his marriage to Edwinna. He was divorced. Edwinna had an earlier marriage and was a widow at the time she met and married Ray. Neither had children in their prior marriage.

Ray and Edwinna was a good-looking couple as you can see from their photographs.

ancestry

1940 United States Federal Census

Name:	Ray O Wagner
Age:	37
Estimated Birth Year:	abt 1903
Gender:	Male
Race:	Negro
Birthplace:	Oklahoma
Marital Status:	Married
Relation to Head of House:	Head
Home in 1940:	Newton, Harvey, Kansas
Street:	West 5th Street
House Number:	721
Farm:	No
Inferred Residence in 1935:	Newton, Harvey, Kansas
Residence in 1935:	Same Place
Sheet Number:	9B
Number of Household in Order of Visitation:	216
Occupation:	Train Porter
House Owned or Rented:	Owned
Value of Home or Monthly Rental if Rented:	3600
Attended School or College:	No
Highest Grade Completed:	College, 3rd year
Hours Worked Week Prior to Census:	40
Class of Worker:	Wage or salary worker in private work
Weeks Worked in 1939:	52
Income:	2184
Income Other Sources:	No

Edwinna at age 21

The Wagners home at 721 West Fifth Street was comfortable. Although Edwinna did not permit Verda to bring in friends very often, Verda had a good childhood.

Ray worked for 39 years for The Atchison, Topeka and Santa Fe Railway System. In addition to the hours he put in for his full-time job, Ray worked three or four part-time jobs over the years. Ray wanted to ensure that he provided the best for his family.

Neither Ray nor Edwinna drank or smoked; however, there was always a bottle of Four Roses whiskey "hidden" in the kitchen. Ray belonged to a card playing social club called the "Dog House." The group would meet once or twice each month. The men played "Penny Poker" and the ladies played "Bridge."

Edwinna was about five years of age when her family moved to Newton, Kansas. Edwinna Willa Cole was born in Perry" Oklahoma on July 13, 1903. She lived there for 12 years after which her family moved to Chicago, Illinois residing there for 13 years. She completed three years of high school. At that time, three year was all required to graduate. She then went on to take a business course. Edwinna worked as a stenographer for a real estate office. She also worked in a lawyer's office. Edwinna studied music as a child with a private tutor. She went to the American Conservatory of Music in Chicago for a semester. She returned to Newton, Kansas in 1934 with her husband, Ray Wagner. She worked for two years during the construction of the airport in Newton, Kansas. Edwinna stopped working in 1944.

Edwinna's physical health was rather poor because she had asthma. In the 1940s and 1950s her asthma attacks were enhanced by her temper tantrums. At times when she could not breathe, someone would have to give her a steroid injection. If Ray was at home at the time of the asthma attack he would give her the injection; otherwise, a neighbor across the street would give the injection. After years of crisis, Edwinna was finally given a small breathing mouth spray that helped relieve the attacks.

Ray and Edwinna moved to Phoenix, Arizona after Ray's retirement from the Santa Fe. Edwinna Johnson Wagner died on October 10, 1983. Her husband, Ray Wagner, died on November 8, 1983 less than 30 days after his wife's death in Phoenix, Arizona.

The Wagners took to their grave that their only child (adopted) was born of White parents.

Edwinna had a sister (Massa Scott) her son Robert died at the age of 12, cause of death unknown.

Ray had two sisters, and two brothers:

Leota Wagner Anderson: deceased,   Her only child, was never able to walk, he was born with "CLUB" feet and legs and was wheelchair bound for life. Because of their religion he did not have any doctor care or surgeries. He died at the age of 30.

Delores Wagner Webb: deceased   Her only son and my ONLY living Wagner relative

Arthur Wagner: deceased   No children

Leroy Wagner   deceased   No children

Ray, Verda and Aunt Leota

FACTS and HOME LIFE

1. Home life in NEWTON with Edwinna and RAY was GOOD and BAD. As most little girls are, I was My DADDY'S LITTLE GIRL" and hated it when he went to work on the train. He was a "GOOD MAN" when Edwinna raised "HELL" with him, he would keep "THE PEACE" by going to work in his garden or feed the chickens and rabbits. (At that time you could have animals in the city limits). He never raised his voice or augured with her.

2. He worked two or three part-time jobs, at the same time, I think to get away from her "BITCHINESS". She was always "MAD" about something.... I remembering staying in my room a lot to stay out of her way and keep her from "GETTING THAT BELT".

3. Edwinna would wait until Ray went to work then say "I WAS LYING" to her, about whatever, then beat me with a leather belt, and put rubbing alcohol on the scars or redness so they did not show when Ray got home. She had an extremely BAD BAD temper and it showed when Ray wasn't around.

4. Ray nor Edwinna smoked or drank but there was always a bottle of "FOUR ROSES" whiskey "hidden" in the kitchen.

5. Ray and Edwinna both belonged to a card playing social club that met once or twice a month. They met at someone's house and once a year they had a joint party. The men played "Penny Poker" and the ladies played "Bridge". I would raid his penny bag when no one was looking and put the pennies in my "PIGGY Bank". Daddy would only shake his head and go earn more at the next "DOG HOUSE" (that is what their group was called) card party.

6. Edwinna ran a tight household budget. When Ray and I would ask for money, her famous words were, "I'm Broke", but she would always have money and dish it out a little at a time, so you would hold on to what she gave you forever and try not to ask her again no time soon.

7. Edwinna was unable to carry a child because her physical health was rather poor due to asthma. In the 40's and 50's her asthma attacks were enhanced by her temper tantrums thus she couldn't get her breath and someone had to give her a steroid injection (shot) so she could breathe again. When Ray was home he would do it but in Ray's absence, I would have to go get a neighbor across the street, Miss Irene, who was some kind of nurse and she would come running to give Edwinna relief. After years of this crisis, Edwinna finally got a small breathing "Mouth spray" to relieve her attacks.

8. Years past and the asthma seemed to disappear but CANCER appeared and two mastectomies had to be performed.

9. When Ray retired from the Santa Fe railroad in 1969, they moved to Phoenix, Arizona and lived there until their death.

10. Cause of death Edwinna CANCER Ray CANCER

11. Edwinna's HOMEGOING (death) October 13, 1983. Age 80

12. Ray's HOMEGOING (death) November 8 1983 (28 days later) Age 82

Early Years

Attending integrated schools and an African-American Church, I was brought up thinking I was in my world, "BLACK". However, about the age of 12, Edwinna told me I was adopted but I didn't know what that meant. Maybe I was naïve and thought no more about it. Edwinna was very strict, so whatever she said or didn't say was okay with me. I grew up an "ONLY" child.

The fact or idea of having another Mama or Dad "Never, Never, Never" crossed my mind.

Me + Mama Edwinna
Age 4-5

Me Daddy + Spat "my dog"
Age 4+5

Early Years

Me + Spat @ age 4-5   Me and my friend
Diana

Me and the Church Ladies

Me & My friend @ a
Wedding

Growing Years

Me Mama & Daddy in
front of my house

62

cousins
+ Uncle
Will

=Verda)
age 3—

Bob Kern
+ Verda
age 3

Verda + Dad

Me and other family

Religious Experience
I grew up in HALL"S CHAPEL AFRICAN AMERICAN ESCOPAIL CHURCH (A.M.E.) one of three small NEGRO Churches in Newton.

Sunday School class @ Hall's Chapel AME Church, Newton, Ks, Verda age 3

Elementary and Middle School

Verda began her education at Lincoln Grade School in Newton, Kansas. The first day of kindergarten, at age 5, does not hold any special memories for Verda. In first through third grades, Verda learned to print her name with BIG LETTERS on lined tablet paper. She remembers that the lines on the paper were "big." Writing and keeping the letters within the lines became very interesting to her because she found copying the letters a difficult task. She remembers reading the popular books during the early years in school. Those books included *Dick and Jane,* and *See Spot* Run. Third through sixth grade subjects included reading, spelling, writing, and arithmetic. Verda's spelling test grades were poor; arithmetic grade was very poor; however, reading was "G" for good. Somehow during her academic struggle, Verda passed to the next grade every year.

There were no school buses to take the student to and from school in Newton, Kansas during the years Verda attended school. If your parents did not take you to school, you had to walk the distance to your designated school. The snow in the winter months could be harsh and Edwinna made Verda walk to school most of the time because Edwinna did not want to drive in the bad weather. Verda did not have any boots. Her feet got cold on many days. Her shoes were thin soled and her socks always got wet during inclement weather. When the weather was bad, she was permitted to eat lunch at Woolworth Company store which was located one block from the school. Normally she walked the six blocks home for lunch. Verda successfully completed elementary school and middle school.

Verda and her family attended Hall's Chapel African American Episcopal (AME) Church. When Verda was 14 years old she was baptized. The church was located at 711 E. 11th Street, Newton, Kansas. Verda enjoyed participating with the youth in church activities.

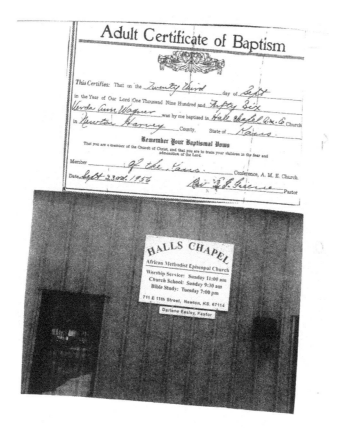

Mama, Grandmother and Me

Me age 10-12

39

High School

Verda attended Newton High School. Verda, an attractive teenager, was permitted to participate in band activities. She played the alto saxophone in the high school marching band and orchestra. The band performed for half-time activities at the high-school football games. The band even performed in the Kansas State Fair.

Newton, Kansas' racial population was 90% White, 5% Negro (the term used for African Americans at that time), and 5% Hispanic. Edwinna's light complexion skin had no bearing on her living in a basic "White" community. Verda had a few Negro friends. Schools in Newton were integrated. Verda graduated from high school in 1960.

Verda attended Newton High School. Verda, an attractive teenager, was permitted to participate in band activities. She played the alto saxophone in the high school marching band and orchestra. The bank performed for half-time activities at the high-school football games. The band even performed in the Kansas State Fair.

Newton, Kansas' racial population was 90% White, 5% Negro (the term used for African Americans at that time), and 5% Hispanic. Edwinna's light complexion skin had no bearing on her living in a basic "White" community. Verda had a few Negro friends. Schools in Newton were integrated. Verda graduated from high school in 1960.

College

Verda attended Bethel College in North Newton for two years. Verda did not venture from Newton because her mother did not want her to leave Newton. Verda's grades, as stated by Verda, were awful. She did not care about the grades because she did not want to be at home. Verda did graduate from Metropolitan College of Denver Colorado with a BS Degree.

Bethel College   Metropolitan College

In the summer of 1962, at the age of 19, Verda left home. She moved to Wichita, Kansas which was twenty miles from Newton. Determined not to spend another minute under Edwinna's roof putting up with her "hateful and controlling" ways. Verda left home carrying one small suitcase. She "slipped away" on a train to Wichita vowing never to live in Newton again. However, as "things" sometimes happen, Verda took a turn that caused her to grow up faster than expected.

Aunt Delane
+ Verda　　　Edwynna

AFTER HIGH SCHOOL and NEWTON

1960-1962

Attended two years of college at Bethel College in North Newton because Edwinna did not want me to go away to college and my grades were awful and I didn't care because I didn't want to be there anyway

The summer of 62, at the age of 19 I left home ..... and moved myself to Wichita 20 miles away thus with one small suitcase, my adult life began. I could not take another minute under Edwinna's roof with her hateful and controlling ways. I had cousins there and could see my boyfriend. I slipped away on a train to Wichita and vowed never to live in Newton never again.

My first boyfriend was named James Templeton. He was a young airman stationed at MCCONNELL AIR FORCE BASE IN Wichita. He and his friends would always come to Newton to the skating rink every Monday night plus he would call me but Edwinna wouldn't let me talk to him and said he was to "Black" for me but we were "Young Lovers" in love.

After moving to Wichita I got pregnant and called my daddy to come and get me, which he did. Edwinna was irate and wanted to put me in a home for "Unwed" mothers but daddy Ray didn't let that happen.

April 1963

My one and only child was born and Edwinna, sent me and baby to live with her sister, my aunt, in Minneapolis Minnesota. After a while, my Aunt got sick and Edwinna came and got her and my baby and took back to Newton to live with her.

I stayed in Minnesota for a couple of more years and began working and collecting "MEN" and "Women friends. I turned 21 and my first drinking experience proved to be a "Mind Blowing","Unforgettable" experience, never to be done in that manner again.

1968

I returned home again in the early summer of 1968, met Kenneth Johnson, who worked on the railroad

during, the summer and married Kenneth in La Junta Colorado later that year.

Kenneth and I moved to Denver and stayed married for four years.

1972

Divorced but stayed in Denver

1973-1977 Started college again at Metropolitan State College in Denver Colorado

Associate of Arts Degree (A.A.) in Drug and Alcohol

Bachelor of Science Degree in Mental Science

November 1978 Met Master Sergeant Trancle Byrd in Denver, Colorado

January 13, 1979 Six weeks later married for the 2nd time still in Denver

1980-1982 Went to Germany as a spouse of a United States Air Force wife

1982-1986 Toyoko Japan

1989-Presant San Antonio Texas been married 36 years and living in Texas 26 years

Birth of a Child

Verda's first boyfriend was James Templeton. He was a young airman stationed at McConnell Air Force Base in Wichita, Kansas. James and his friends would come to Newton to the skating rink every Monday night. He would call Verda; however, Edwinna would not let Verda talk to him and said he was "too Black" for Verda. After moving to Wichita, Verda got pregnant. She called her daddy to come and pick her up, which he did. Edwinna was irate and wanted to put Verda in a home for "unwed mothers." Daddy would not permit that to happen

In April 1963, Verda's gave birth to a daughter. Edwinna sent Verda and her daughter to live with her aunt (Edwinna's sister) in Minneapolis, Minnesota. Edwinna did not want her unmarried daughter living in the house because having a "bastard" baby was not acceptable. Verda and the baby had not been living with the aunt very long when the aunt became ill. At that point, Edwinna came and took the baby to Newton to live with her and Ray Wagner. Eventually Edwinna and Ray decided to raise Verda's daughter.

Hazel Lamm
Verda Bill & Walker
Tyona

Tyona 1966

Tyona 12 yrs old 11-15

My Daughter
My Mom & Me

Road Trip to Newton For Old Time Sake

March 2015: *For memory and recall of EARLY and MIDDLE years (1942-1950)*

The journey from San Antonio TX to Newton was an informational trip because I had not seen the modern town and needed to refresh my memory of my "HOME TOWN". Fifty miles away the signs began to read welcome to KANSAS thus Newton was not far away. Wichita came first then 20 minutes later came Newton.

The migration of the RUSSIAN-GERMAN MENNONITE culture in Newton begin with a small delegation of Mennonites that toured the land that the railroad had bought. The newly acquired land was agricultural land and created a civilized urban environment that had changed from an unruly and wild frontier Cowtown. Their culture was liberal and industrious They were considered as one of the best classes of citizens

In 1880's a group of Mennonites felt they needed a church college. A Mennonite immigrant and Newton businessman, surveyed the open prairie and it became NORTH NEWTON and Bethel college was established.

Bethel college became charted in 1887, and began building their campus. The students were up at five in the morning and in bed by ten at night. Each student worked two hours a day at a campus job. Student conduct was strictly monitored. Men and women were not allowed to be in the library during the same evenings: with their general education program was geared to liberal arts and sciences and high academic ability. High quality education was expected for the "WHOLE" person.

Sept. 1960- June 1963   I myself (Verda) attended Bethel College

A peek into the past college years was an opportunity to see why I didn't like "THAT" college at "THAT" time.

The HISTORY of Newton goes like this:

Newton had been a cow town, with a rowdy reputation and one of the wickedest cow towns in the west.

Bernhard Warkentin encouraged 5,000 Mennonites to migrate to Kansas and they brought seeds of hard wheat to plant and harvest. The main street was established and new business began to boom and Kansas became known as the WHEAT state.

The first passenger train arrived July 10, 2017, and Newton began to thrive with new business.

It was named after Newton Massachusetts, home of some of the Santa Fe stockholders.. In 1972 the western terminal for the Santa Fe and the railhead for the Chisholm Trail was established here.

At that time Newton prohibited the running of buffalo and other wild animals. And became the middle division dispatching headquarters for the Santa Fe until the mid-1980's.

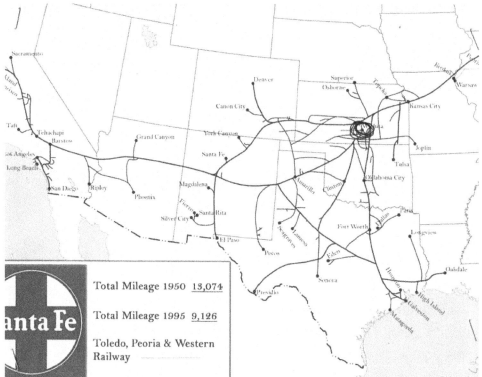

In 1995 the Santa Fe railroad merged with the Burlington Northern Railroad, and now named as the Burlington Northern Railroad.

The only trains that go through Newton now is the AMTRACK:

arrive at 2:45 A.M. going west…#3

arrive at 2:59 A.M. going east…#4

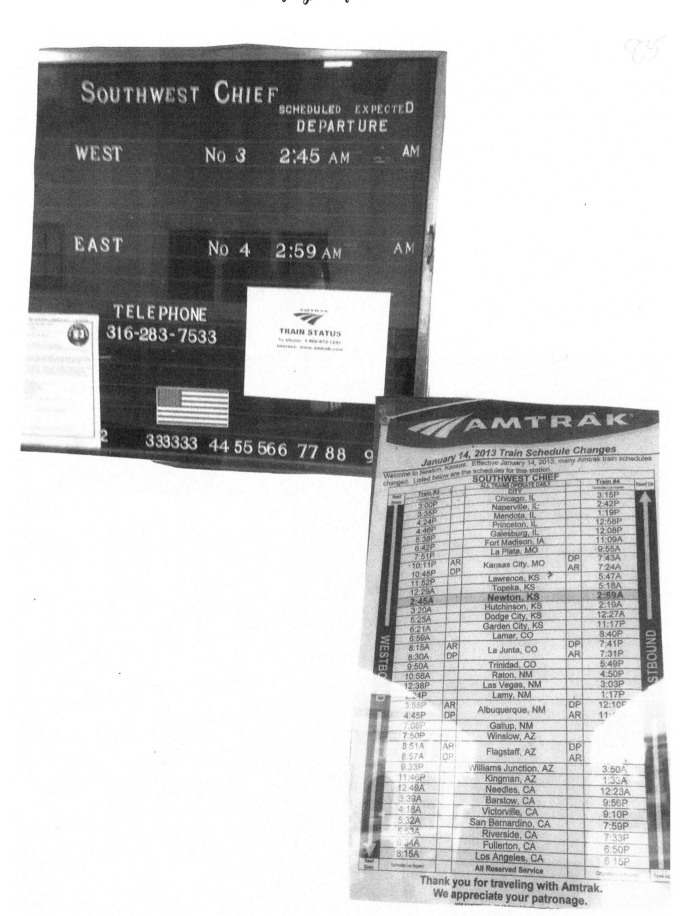

The next stop in downtown Newton was the historic old Santa Fe Depot. I found an open door on the side of the building and began to explore the inside. The interior of the building was not even recognized with all the changes. Only small train waiting area was all that remained by the front door. The empty waiting area was a small and no one was selling tickets to nowhere. It was so disappointing to NOT see the "GHOST" trains of decades ago.

In 1984 the Santa Fe railroad was found guilty of DISCRIMINATION resulting from the railroad's segregated job structure for brakeman (WHITES) and train porters. (NEGROES/blacks) The porter's tip's were more than their monthly salary from the railroad. A train job was one of stability and held high social prestige in the African-American community. After twenty years of fighting for equal rights, my dad Ray, died one year before this SUPREME COURT CASE was settled. My dad, Ray Wagner, made $250.00 a month plus tips. Ray started working for the Santa Fe in the 1930 and after 39 years retired at age 68.

Downtown Newton has no parking meters so you just parallel park, get out of your car and shop.

There are NO city buses thus the metal street benches were for "REST STOPS….. NOT Bus Stops

Woolworth's lunch counter did NOT serve the NEGRO train porters

In 1957 the first integrated restaurant opened and welcomed the African American railroad porters and gave them a place to eat.

My evenings were spent just riding around and "LOOKING". The house I grew up in, on the corner of west 5th, looked still the same, but seemed smaller.

My grandparents, Bertha and Simeon Wagner house on E.6th street had been empty for many years and often times homeless people would stay there on cold nights.

Simeon A. Wagner

Simeon Avon Wagner, retired Santa Fe railroad employee of 515 East Sixth street, died Sunday afternoon at Bethel Deaconess hospital. He had been a patient in the hospital for five days.

Mr. Wagner, who had lived in this community for 35 years, was born July 9, 1878 in Missouri and was past 71 years of age. He was a member of thee A. M. E. church and of Rising Sun lodge No. 69 A. F. and A. M.

Mr. Wagner is survived by his wife, Bertha Edith, of the home; three daughters, Mrs. Ieota Anderson and Mrs. Velora Campbell of Kansas City, Kans., Mrs. Delores Webb of Minneapolis, Minn., and three sons, Ray O. Wagner of Newton, Leon O. Wagner and William R. Wakner, both of Los Angeles, Calif.

He also leaves three sisters, Mrs. Edward Hill and Mrs. Allen Walker of Kansas City, Kans., Mrs. Charles Taylor of Tacoma, Wash.; three brothers, William F. Wagner of Newton, Ernest M. Wagner of Albuquerque, N. M., Meritt Wagner of Sacramento, Calif., eight great grandchildren and a number of grandchildren, nieces and nephews.

Funeral services will be conducted Wednesday morning at ten o'clock at the A. M. E. church. Rev. Walter Lillard will officiate and burial will be in Greenwood cemetery. Friends may see Mr. Wagner Tuesday evening at the Draper Funeral chapel.

Deaths

Mrs. Bertha Wagner

Mrs. Bertha Edith Wagner, 79, former Newton resident, died Wednesday of a heart attack in Los Angeles.

Mrs. Wagner, who formerly resided at 315 E. 6th, had been living with a daughter in Minneapolis, Minn., and was visiting a son in Los Angeles at the time of her death. She was a member of the Second Baptist Church here.

She was married July 9, 1908 at Enid, Okla., to Simeon A. Wagner, who died in 1948.

Survivors include three daughters, Mrs. Leota Anderson and Mrs. Velora Campbell, both of Kansas City, Kas., and Mrs. Delores Webb of Minneapolis; three sons, Ray O. of Newton, LeRoy O. of Los Angeles and William R. of Los Angeles; eight grandchildren, nine great grandchildren and a sister.

The body is being returned to Newton and arrangements will be announced by Draper's Funeral Home.

The last day of my "ROAD TRIP" was to HALSTEAD KANSAS, 8 miles away, "Just to See" the old hospital my mother EDWINNA would go to for any serious medical issues. Signs along the way read FOR SALE TORNADO SHELTERS. Now sixty years later, A BIG EMPTY BUILDING that was never used for anything else sits in the middle of "MAYBERRY" with no stop lights, cobblestone town with the population of 2,000.

Coming home

Verda Byrd looks through childhood photos. Byrd was adopted by a Newton family nd reconnected with her birth siblings — scattered across the United States — after 70 years. Ashley Bergner/Newton Kansan

y Ashley Bergner
ewton Kansan
ABergner_Kansan

sted Mar. 25, 2015 at 1:00 PM

ewton, Kan.

Family is a gift Verda Byrd certainly doesn't take for granted. Given up for adoption at the age of one in 1944, she grew up as an only child in Newton. Even though her adoptive family was loving and kind, she always wondered about her birth family. Now, 70 years later, she's finally reconnecting with her birth siblings, who are scattered across the United States.

The Kansan first covered Byrd's story in April 2014. Byrd — who currently lives in San Antonio, Texas — recently returned to Newton for a visit to collect more details about her past for an upcoming biography.

"Newton was the beginning," she said.

And it's been quite a story. Byrd was born "Jeanette Beagle" to a poor family in the Kansas City area. Byrd's birth mother, Daisy Beagle, had a difficult life. At age 27, she found herself raising five children alone when her husband left home to buy milk and never returned. Beagle tried to find employment but was seriously injured in a trolley accident. Unable to care for all her children, one-year-old Byrd was turned over for adoption.

Ray and Edwinna Wagner gave Byrd a new home. Her adoptive father worked on the Santa Fe railroad as a porter, commonly running from Newton to Oklahoma and Newton to Kansas City. It was through his work that he got in touch with a children's home in Kansas City, which led to the adoption of Byrd.

Byrd lived at 721 W. Fifth St. in Newton and attended Lincoln Elementary School. She was the first black child to go to the McKinley swimming pool. She said segregation unfortunately still was a reality in Newton, and racism could be found in the community, even in experiences she heard about in the Woolsworths store.

She remembers attending Sunday school at Hall's Chapel AME.

"I grew up in that church," she said.

She graduated from Newton High School in 1960 and attended Bethel College from 1961 to 1962.

Byrd is struck by the contrast between her birth parents and her adoptive parents. The Beagles were drifters living in poverty, while the Wagners were an affluent black family — which was in the minority in Newton at the time, she said.

Byrd began a serious search for her birth family in October 2013. Four out of the 10 Beagle siblings are still living, and Byrd now has met her other three sisters, who reside in Texas, Nebraska and Florida. They met together for the first time June 21, 2014. Three of the four siblings were able to spend last Christmas together and visited the grave of their birth mother.

"I have been so overwhelmed this past year," she said. "... The meet and greet is developing into sisterhood."

It was time to leave Newton and our final meal in Kansas was at Newalls truck stop but there was an antiquate and collectable store at next door and of course I found "STUFF" that would be returned to Texas with me. Leaving Kansas and hoping not to return NO TIME SOON.

Marriage/Divorce

In 1969 Verda returned to Newton where she met and married Kenneth Johnson, a summer employee of the Santa Fe railroad. After the summer, Verda and Kenneth moved to Denver, Colorado. After four years of marriage, the couple divorced. Verda stayed in Denver. She attended Metropolitan State College earning a Bachelor of Science Degree in Mental Health.

After the divorce, Verda remained in Denver, Colorado. Verda worked for the City of Denver, Colorado as a drug and alcohol counselor. Verda remained a City employee. It was during her tenure with the City that she met Trancle Lamar Byrd.

Second Marriage

In 1979 Verda married Trancle Lamar Byrd (T. Byrd), an active-duty Air Force enlisted person. At that time, they lived in Denver, Colorado. T. Byrd was stationed at Lowry AFB. Verda experienced living in many places, different cultures. From Denver, the Byrd's were transferred to Ramstein AFB. They lived in Germany four years. During the time, they were stationed in Germany, Verda's parents died. The military then transferred them to Luke AFB, Phoenix, Arizona. From Phoenix, they went to Tokyo, Japan. Verda enjoyed the culture and mingling with the Japanese culture. In her home, she has a folding wall made of soap stone with Japanese paper painted on the canvas. There is also a wall picture made of Japanese soap stone   Near the end of T. Byrd's active duty military service, he was transferred to Randolph AFB, Universal City, Texas. Universal City is a small community just east of San Antonio. Verda's husband retired from the military; they reside in Converse, Texas.

PICTURES THROUGH THE YEARS

photo by
bill watson

09/13/2008

Reva going to Church

FINDING FAMILY AND ME
The Search to Find "Me"

October-November 1983. Ray and Edwinna Wagner died 28 days apart. Cleaning up their house and going through cabinet drawers and closets Verda came across the adoption documents from the Kansas City Adoption Court with the name of Jeanette Beagle on it. The date on the document was June 5, 1947 (almost 40 years old).

She put it away and never really thought about it anymore because being a military wife, her life was going in opposite directions and she was not really interested and didn't care what the document said.

Thirty plus years passed and cleaning up her own house, she came across it again and this time was different because she had time and wanted to discover who Jeanette Beagle was.

Verda said "I need to find out who this person is." "I should do this NOW or NEVER" so with a "LEAP OF FAITH" she set out to find JEANETTE BEAGLE.

August 13, 2013. Verda sent a request letter for information about Jeanette to the Circuit Court of Jackson County, Missouri at Kansas City with the case number on it.

October 24, 2013. Received letter from the court authorizing a searcher to search for the biological parents of the adoptee and to initiate investigative steps for Jeanette Beagle. Verda chose Sandra Sperrazza for this task because the STATE of MISSOURI could NOT give any information to me directly; but first, they had to prove that the "BIRTH" parents were deceased.

November 7, 2013. Letter sent to Sandy Sperrazza from the court authorizing her to initiate a search for the biological parents of Verda Wagner.

January 24, 2014.ORDER from the CIRCUIT COURT OF JACKSON COUNTY, MISSOURI, AT KANSAS CITY FAMILY COURT DIVISION. IT WAS ORDERED that the PETITION to Obtain ADOPTION Records for release of information regarding the biological mother Daisy Beagle Pierce and biological father Earl Beagle is granted and that Verda Ann Wagner Byrd shall be provided with a copy of her Court adoption which included her name change from JEANETTE BEAGLE to VERDA ANN WAGNER.

February 2014. Verda Byrd receives HER ADOPTION DOCUMENTS.

CIRCUIT COURT OF JACKSON COUNTY, MISSOURI
FAMILY COURT DIVISION
625 East 26th Street
Kansas City, Missouri 64108
http://www.family-court.org

Rosalee Schottel

Family Court Services   (816) 435-4788

ADOPTION INFORMATION REQUEST

NAME _VERDA WAGNER (BYRD)_

ADDRESS _____

CITY, STATE, ZIP CODE _CONVERSE TX 78109_

TELEPHONE _210-566-4443_

To identify the court adoption file, please complete the following to the best of your knowledge:

COURT ADOPTION FILE NUMBER _15301_   *Birth Date'd 9-27-42*

BIOLOGICAL NAME _Jeanette Beagle._

ADOPTIVE NAME _Verda WAGNER_

DATE OF BIRTH _9-27-42_

ADOPTIVE PARENTS _RAY O WagNeR and EdwiNNA WAGNeR_

BIOLOGICAL PARENTS _____

Please check appropriate item(s):

_____ I request **non-identifying information** regarding the biological parents (physical description, nationality, religious background, type of employment, reason for adoption, education, ethnic origin and medical history, if known). There is a **fee of $50.00** for receipt of non-identifying information. Payable by **money order only**, to Jackson County Family Court.

_✓_ I request **identifying information** regarding my biological parents. I understand this would require locating them and any such search must be conducted by an agency approved by the court or otherwise permitted by law.

_____ **Other** (please explain) _____

Aug. 13 2013   _Verda Byrd_
DATE   SIGNATURE

Please include proof of identity such as a copy of your BIRTH CERTIFICATE, DRIVERS'S LICENSE, or SOCIAL SECURITY CARD, ETC.

Amended birth Certificates Are available through Vital Records.
816-513-L309

CIRCUIT COURT OF JACKSON COUNTY, MISSOURI
FAMILY COURT DIVISION
625 East 26th Street
Kansas City, Missouri 64108

Rosalee Schottel
Legal Assistant

(816) 435-4788

October 24, 2013

Verda Byrd
7703 Rio Blanco
Converse, TX 78109

RE: Adoption File #15301

Dear Ms. Byrd:

I have reviewed the adoption file. Unfortunately we have only the birth parents' names. Therefore, I requested a copy of your original birth certificate to review for search purposes only. We now know the birth parents' age and state of birth.

We can provide this information to a searcher, so she can search for the family in the old census records. If the search is successful in finding proof the parents are deceased, we will then be able to release the information that the new legislation allows released.

The Court can provide information about the birth parents to a searcher but not directly to you, the decision on whether or not to retain a searcher is your decision. Should you decide to retain a searcher I have enclosed a list of agencies.

If you have any questions or concerns, please contact me at (816) 435-4788.

Sincerely,

Rosalee Schottel

Rosalee Schottel

Enclosure

1-24-2014
pr phone call
Birth info will be sent last wk of Jan 2014
end of next wk. Last wk of

CIRCUIT COURT OF JACKSON COUNTY, MISSOURI
FAMILY COURT DIVISION
625 East 26th Street
Kansas City, Missouri 64108

Rosalee Schottel   rosalee.schottel@courts.mo.gov
(816) 435-4788

November 7, 2013

Sandra Sperrazza
6429 Mendelssohn
Hopkins, MN 55343-8424

Re: Verda Byrd
    DOB: 09-27-1942
    Adoption File:#15301
    Adoptive Parents: Ray & Edwina Wagner

Dear Ms. Sperrazza:

This letter authorizes you to search for the biological parents of the above-referred adoptee and to request that you initiate the investigative steps directed by Missouri law, (Section 453.121.5 RSMO).

Please be advised that this letter does not authorize you to divulge any identifying information to the adoptee at this time. Such authorization may be granted by a court order after we have received your investigative report along with the biological parents' consent.

Missouri law requires that your investigative report be filed with the Court within (3) months. In this case your report is due at the Court on or about February 7, 2014. If a search requires additional time, the Court will grant up to a (3) month extension after a continuance has been requested and granted.

If you have any questions or concerns, please contact me at (816) 435-4788. Thank you in advance for your assistance and cooperation.

Sincerely,

Rosalee Schottel

Rosalee Schottel
Enclosures

IN THE CIRCUIT COURT OF JACKSON COUNTY, MISSOURI, AT KANSAS CITY
FAMILY COURT DIVISION

IN RE THE ADOPTION OF:

Jeanette Beagle
Verda Ann Wagner   ADOPTION FILE No. 15301

Date of Birth: 09-27-1942

ORDER

Upon review of the Petition to Obtain Adoption Records and Pursuant to Senate Bill No. 351, the court finds the following: (1) Petitioner's biological parents' are deceased. (2) The adoption file provides proof of death of the biological parents, which would warrant release of identifying information from the above-referenced adoption file.

IT IS HEREBY ORDERED that the Petition to Obtain Adoption Records for release of identifying information regarding the biological mother, Daisy Beagle Pierce, born August 5, 1915, and died September 18, 2002 and biological father, Earl Beagle, died January 5, 1988, is granted, and that Verda Ann Wagner Byrd shall be provided with a copy of her Court adoption file record.

IT IS SO ORDERED.

1-24-14
_____
DATE

_____
Judge John Torrence
Administrative Judge
Family Court Division

Copies to:

Verda Byrd
7703 Rio Blanco
Converse, TX 78109

210-566-4443

Rosalee Schottel, Legal Assistant, Family Court Division

December 12, 2013

To: Rosalee Schottel
    Adoption Investigator
    625 East 26th Street
    Kansas City, Mo. 64108-2719

From: Sandra L. Sperrazza
      6429 Mendelssohn Lane
      Hopkins, MN 55343-8424

ADOPTION SEARCH REPORT TO THE JACKSON COUNTY FAMILY COURT

Adoptee: Verda Wagner Byrd
         7703 Rio Blanco
         Converse, Texas 78109
         File # 15301
         D.O.B. 09-27-1942

Birthmother: Daisey Beagle Pierce
             Deceased

Birthfather: Earl Beagle
             Deceased

Referral Information:
On November 7, 2013, the Jackson County Family Court requested that a search be done to locate the deaths of the birthparents for the above mentioned adoptee.
Pursuant to her request, and following the steps as directed by Section 453.121.5 RSMo., the following information was found.

In Byrd's search to "find me," she set out to find the living siblings.   She located three sisters, Sybil Panko of Merritt Island, Florida; Debbie Romero, Dallas, Texas; and, Kathryn Rouillard of Omaha, Nebraska. Byrd sent a certified copy of a handwritten letter and copy of adoption papers with Daisy Beagle's signature affixed to Sybil Panko. On February 24, 2014, Sybil Panko called her sister Debbie Romero in Dallas, Texas telling her that she had received a letter from a lady claiming to be their sister. And, that the sister had been placed in adoption by their mother, Daisy. When Daisy Beagle's daughters were growing up, they remembered their mother's stories about the baby girl she had given up for adoption. They also remembered Daisy talking about the "hard days" trying to raise five children in Kansas City in the early 1940s. Daisy Beagle had often wondered if the child she had given up for adoption had a good life.

The first communication Verda got was from Debbie who called her phone number and from their conversation, there was no doubt that they are sisters. Romero says, "I know she is my sister, I don't need a DNA test." Later in the day, the third sister, Kathryn, was called and a three-way conversation ensued.

On February 27, 2014 Verda talked one-on-one with Kathryn and her other new found sisters. The sisters spent hours on the telephone talking about why they had gotten separated from "Mama Daisy."

By this time, Verda had begun to reach information overload. She thought, "Have I found me." Verda, growing up an only child did not interact with siblings as her friends who had sisters and brothers in the home. We can say Verda was beginning, at age 71, to really enjoy the "childish feeling" of having siblings that she could "reach out and touch."

Verda is beginning to feel, "I have really found me." Now is the time for her to get together with her new-found family.

HER MYSTERY HAS BEEN SOLVED. HER RACE AND CULTURE had instantly changed!!!! NOT EVERYONE WILL UNDERSTAND "MY" JOURNEY, THAT'S OK. VERDA SAYS, 'I'M HERE TO LIVE MY LIFE NOT TO MAKE EVERYONE UNDERSTAND."

In August, all three of Byrd's surviving siblings, spread across the country, rendezvoused in San Antonio, For Panko, the union was 70 years in the making, as for the others a first opportunity to hug Byrd. Rouillard recollected her mother speaking of a child she had to give up.

"Mother had told me she had a daughter that she put up for adoption and always wondered if she was all right," she said. As Byrd learned more about her first family, she asked why they moved so often and was told their parents were "drifters."

Verda told me the level of excitement of meeting the first sister in Dallas, Texas was overwhelming. She had provided pictures and knew how her sister looked but meeting your sister, at age 71, was not going to be easy. On the scale from 1 – 10 her anxiety, she says, was "75".

EPILOGUE

On interview Verda gave me the following that means so much to her as she moves forward with her life. "Love the life you live. Live the life you love. We live what we 'learn.'"
Jeanette B. (White birth parents) or Verda B. (Negro adopted parents)

Verda grew up as an only child. Edwinna had a sister; no children. Ray had two sisters. One sister, Leota Wagner Anderson, had a child who never walked; totally wheelchair bound. He died as a young man, age 30. Ray's other sister, Delores Wagner Webb had one son, Curtis, Verda's only living cousin. We provide these facts to let you know that Verda grew up in a community in a very small family. Family activities and memorable activities mostly involved going to church every Sunday and holiday dinners.

Verda said the fact that she found out she was born of White parents really didn't matter but her MENTAL acceptance of the WHITE word and RACE gave her Posttraumatic Stress Disorder (PTSD). I quote Verda, "The KKK and BURNING CROSSES flashed in my mind and I developed "Emotional Numbness."My biological family was not even thought of until later." End Quote.

Verda told me the level of excitement of meeting the first sister in Dallas, Texas was overwhelming. She had been provided pictures and knew how the sister looked. Verda said on a scale of 1-10, she felt "75." She does not know if her sister had the same level of excitement.
Verda felt the same level of excitement when "Daisy's Daughters" met in her home in San Antonio, Texas. The meet and greet in San Antonio was exciting.

When I asked Verda if she was still in contact with her biological sisters she said "NO" and "I don't really know why." Her sister Sybil died in September 2016 and all communication among the sisters STOPPED which included texting and phone calls. They requested that she not attend her sister's funeral. She was not with her sister when she died. She feels maybe they promised her (the sister) "never to talk to me again. I do not know, but her wishes were that I not come."

Finding family was an exhilarating experience for Verda. Knowing what she knows now, she would do it all over again. In closing, Verda said "I was never upset to begin with. The good Lord and love from both sets of parents led me on this exciting and wonderful "finding me" journey. I don't know of any other way I could have done it. I 'Stepped out on Faith' and thank the Lord for all blessings."

It may seem insignificant to be born of "WHITE" parents but it had a "HUGE" controversy in my life.

The morality of giving a minor child a "GOOD and LOVING" home was the basic cause for adoption and also the fundamental cause for "FOSTER CARE".

Inappropriate placement in the "EARLY 40's" and the absence of "RACIAL MATCHING" for children, up for adoption," Did not Exist".

Question……Was that a misdemeanor, felony, or just "Rigged"?

This historical decision has affected my whole life. There was no protesting "ADOPTION WAS JUST DONE".

I am a RACIAL SURVIVOR and cherish my life…..

THANK YOU LORD FOR ALL MY EARTHLY BLESSINGS

LOVE THE LIFE YOU LOVE
And
LIVE THE LIFE YOU LOVE

CPSIA information can be obtained
at www.ICGtesting.com
Printed in the USA
BVHW060446251022
650211BV00005B/54